Simon
EASTERBY
Easter's Rising

with Alun Gibbard

y Lolfa

First impression: 2011

© Copyright Simon Easterby and Y Lolfa Cyf., 2011

The publishers wish to acknowledge the support of
Cyngor Llyfrau Cymru

Cover design: Y Lolfa
Cover photograph: Getty Images

ISBN: 978 184771 343 8

FSC

Published and printed in Wales
on paper from well maintained forests
by Y Lolfa Cyf., Talybont, Ceredigion SY24 5HE
website www.ylolfa.com
e-mail ylolfa@ylolfa.com
tel 01970 832 304
fax 832 782

Contents

THANKS TO

Alun Gibbard for his patience in putting this book together

Y Lolfa for giving me the opportunity to tell my story

*Sarra, Soffia and Ffredi
and all my family for their support*

All the medics and physios who've kept me in one piece over the years!

1

Which Country?

"THERE WAS A call for you while you were out Si, some bloke called Clive."

Matt Cardey, the New Zealander who played full-back for the Scarlets, shared a house with me in Llanelli, both of us having signed for the town's world-famous rugby club at around the same time.

"Clive? Who the hell is Clive? Did he say Clive who?"

"Yeah, I think so, I wrote it down somewhere."

Matt is an extremely laid-back kind of guy, bordering on the horizontal! Eventually, the relevant piece of paper was found and I could read for myself which Clive had phoned me – Woodward! It was a bit of a shock to say the least.

"You sure this is right? It is Woodward, is it? Do you know who he is Matt?"

"Umm... no, who is the guy?"

"The England coach, mate!"

"Oh sweet, man!"

Yes, I suppose it was 'sweet' of him to ring. 'Wow' was another word that shot through my mind on realising who'd phoned. But I wondered what he wanted. Why had he tried to contact me? As time went on, the obvious answer dawned on me. There was really only one reason why an international coach would ring a player. But it's not the kind of thought you allow to break loose, just in case. So I kept my thoughts contained as much as I could until I actually got to speak to the man himself.

That happened a little later the same day.

"I've been watching you play in the Heineken group stage games you've been involved with so far, and I'd like to ask you to join the England squad."

So there it was. An invitation to play for England. He'd obviously done his homework and knew that I was English born. I had only just joined the Scarlets in the summer of 1999. This call was in January 2000, so he hadn't had a lot of time to see me play or know much about me. I'd played in games against Bourgoin and Wasps in my first Heineken campaign. Wasps had beaten us comfortably at Adams Park, but we had beaten them comfortably at Stradey. We'd won both games against Bourgoin.

I asked him if he knew that I had already played for Ireland A and under-21s. He said that he did but that didn't preclude me from playing at a senior level for another country. Since that Ireland A game against Canada at Ravenhill in 1997, I hadn't heard another word from the Irish rugby camp. So what was I to do?

"We would like to take you on the England tour to South Africa in the summer and give you a chance out there, if you accept the offer to play for England."

This was really good to hear in what was my first season in top-flight rugby. But, maybe not being at home when Clive Woodward telephoned was actually a blessing. It gave me time to think before speaking to him. As a result, when I was confronted with his request, there was no big decision to make really. There was no need to ask for time to think before giving my answer, which I probably would have done had I answered his initial call.

"No thank you, Mr Woodward, I'm going to stick with Ireland."

He accepted my decision and added that if ever I changed my mind, or if Ireland didn't come after me, then I could call him back at any time. But I'd had no aspirations to play for England at all since putting on the Irish jersey for both the under-21 and A teams. From that moment on, I had made my mind up that Ireland was the country I wanted to play for and this invitation, even a personal call from Clive Woodward, wasn't going to make me change my mind, and neither was the complete silence from the Irish camp for three years prior to his call going to sway me in another direction.

If Ireland hadn't picked me ever again, then the decision could well have backfired on me. Saying no could have destined me to the international wilderness. Ireland might not have contacted me at all, Woodward might not have said yes if I went back to him cap in hand. There might have been the outside chance of playing for Wales through residency if I stayed with the Scarlets or any other Welsh region, for long enough. Despite all this, I certainly didn't want to hedge my bets and say yes to England in order to get a game for their A side and then hop back to Ireland if they came looking again. It was possible to do that in those days and some players did keep their options open in such a way. But for me, I had set out my stall and was going to stand behind it, come what may.

People have asked me since if I regretted the decision in light of what Woodward's team went on to achieve in the 2003 World Cup. The answer is a simple 'no'. So many things would have had to fall into place before I would have taken my place on the pitch for that final. England's victory came more than three years after the phone call. And, in that period, they'd developed their Holy Trinity of Dallaglio, Back and Hill, as well.

I was born in England, in Harrogate, Yorkshire to an Irish mother and an English father. So when I was growing up, I would watch both England and Ireland internationals without any sense of loyalty to one more than the other. If I was in Ireland with my Irish family, I would automatically support Ireland. If in Yorkshire with my dad, I would support England. I played for Yorkshire Schools, North of England Schools and I'd had an England Schools trial in Nottingham. I played for Yorkshire under-21s and the North of England under-21s also.

But, at the same time as all this was happening, the Irish Exiles came knocking on my door. They were, at the time, like a fifth province playing games against the four Irish regions: Ulster, Munster, Connacht and Leinster. Their players were mostly from London Irish and top established teams like Wasps. My brother Guy played for the Exiles. I played for their under-21 team a few times and that's what led on to my playing for the Ireland under-21 team at the Six Nations in 1996.

In so many ways, the easy option would have been to stay with England. It was a system I understood and was part of. I knew the lads on other teams. Going to Ireland would mean walking in to a dressing room as a complete stranger and taking my place alongside lads who knew each other well. The minute I decided that it was Ireland for me, I was out of my comfort zone in a big way. I was an outsider. What doesn't help is that it takes me a long time to develop skills to get on with people I don't know all that well, because, whatever it may look like on the pitch, I am quite a shy person. So, staying with England would have been easier on that score as well. The pull of the Irish must have been quite strong for me to fly in the face of such obvious personal obstacles.

By the time I'd left school, two paths were firmly laid down: one leading to England and the other across the waters to Ireland, the two crossing on the rugby pitch. Securing an identity was an issue from day one. Many have tried to label me over the years, with newspaper phrases varying from 'Irish Yorkshireman', 'Englishman', 'English-born Irishman' to the straightforward 'Irish international' and, occasionally, 'Irishman'. Now of course, there's another twist because I've lived in Wales for so many years and have a Welsh family. So 'naturalised Welshman' is added to the mix. What am I then? To which country do I belong?

For Clive Woodward there was only one answer. But in so many ways, it hasn't always been that clear-cut. Some of my Irish team mates haven't always understood why an Englishman with an English accent played for Ireland and have made their feelings about that known. Then, there's the matter of trying to win over the Irish press and through them, the supporters. That certainly wasn't easy and it took a long time. To be honest, I'm not sure that people in my situation are ever fully accepted and integrated and I don't think that I'm regarded as a full Irishman, even to this day.

An English accent doesn't always help when you

move to Wales either, as I found out when I joined the Scarlets. In both these Celtic countries, there's still a stigma attached to having a Saxon accent. It takes time to break down such perceptions. For me, making the proud choice to play for Ireland doesn't in any way deny or denounce my Englishness. As a monoglot myself, I'm also proud that my children are being brought up to speak Welsh as well as English.

I seem to remember from my Catholic upbringing that the Old Testament refers to a three-corded rope as being the strongest. If that's the case, the three cords of my life, Irish, English and Welsh, have woven together to make me what I am today and, as I have come to know myself while writing my story, they have made me all the stronger for it.

2

A Yorkshire Boyhood

THE SIGNS WERE there early on in my life that rugby might be the sport for me. I came into this world a little over a whopping 10lbs. All indications therefore pointed to me being a prop in the good old-fashioned sense of the word. That's how things stayed as well for the first few years of my life, earning me the not-so-kind nicknames readily associated with rotund little boys. I think that 'tank' was the one that stuck the most and fell into common usage more than the others, although 'podge' was a close contender too. That's the picture that would come into the mind of anyone who knew me when they thought of the young Simon Easterby running around a farmyard near Harrogate.

The family farmhouse was an 18th-century stone-building which had been in my father's family since the end of the Second World War. Kirkby Grange is about twenty-five minutes from Harrogate and is as much rural Yorkshire as it's possible to be, set as it is, in the rolling countryside near the small village of Kirkby Wharfe, two miles south of Tadcaster. Whatever picture people might have of an idyllic childhood, the setting for my formative years would be in many people's minds. I don't think we – my brother Guy and sister Debs – were ever indoors for much more than the time we spent asleep in bed. There was no central heating in the house, so that was never a reason to stay indoors! It was out in the country air from sunup to sundown. Being able to open the front door and have free access to acres and acres of fields was something I absolutely loved. Every field was a different playground; every tree had its own potential in the minds of three lively children.

As kids we helped a lot on the farm, if indeed it can be called help when you've only been walking for a year or two! The farm reared sheep but it was also a horse breeding stud. Animals, therefore, have been important to me from day one. A really early memory is of little lambs, either abandoned at birth or whose mothers were ill, being brought into the house to be wrapped up in old clothing and placed in the bottom of the Aga, to warm them up so that they would survive the first few hours of their fragile lives. At other times a lamb might be ill or suffering a broken leg and we would then enclose them in the back garden near the house. Feeding these lambs by hand was something I treasured.

The three of us shared a horse as well. Dandy was hard work, to say the least! I think his best years were behind him when we bought him. If we're talking human years, I'm sure that Dandy would have been about 75, set in his ways, and not particularly keen on three kids jumping all over him and screaming to high heaven. And like any 75-year-old man who might have three children using him as a climbing frame incessantly, Dandy did get annoyed with us quite often! We all had a go at learning to ride a horse properly, although I must say that it was Debs who was best at it. Guy and I gave it a fair go but, as we grew up, other things started to take over, like rugby and cricket. I guess we didn't fully appreciate what we had on our doorstep at the time, and now, with the glorious benefit of hindsight, and considering my current love of horse racing, I can see that I was presented with plenty of opportunities to do far more than I actually did.

We had to fit school into this idyllic rural life, of course, and we attended Saxton Church of England school. During my sister's time at the school, there were only about 20 pupils there in total. By the time I'd left Saxton, the numbers had increased to about 40. But, numbers having doubled or not, it was still a small rural school. The food there was out of this world, which did nothing to diminish my appetite or my size! The school cook would be given fresh local produce by the farmers in the area every single day and she would cook all her nutritious meals from scratch. It all did very nicely to feed the 'tank'! And, of course, my mum always put our own farm produce to good use at home. That was true whatever the circumstances were. I remember splitting my finger open one day after playing on the tractor. I still have the scar to this day. But my mum, as concerned as she was about the injury itself, made sure that I ate all my tea first – although it probably wasn't even a meal time – before taking me to the hospital, just in case I wouldn't have any food (or food of any use) while I was there. My finger was nearly falling off, but at least I had a full stomach!

I didn't actually start school at the same age as everyone else either. I think it was a case of being held back by my mum who was reluctant to let the last chick fly the nest. I was, as a result, six years old when I started primary school, but I don't think that my development suffered a great deal as a result! An extra year on the farm was more than welcome. As I was the youngest, I was already used to being on the farm on my own more than my brother or sister anyway, because they were away at boarding school. By the time I did start at Saxton, Guy had already left to go to Ampleforth Catholic boarding school and Debs had left to go to a school in York. So, I was six and king of the farm, a reign that would last for about four years!

A huge part of the idyllic childhood I referred to earlier surrounded sports. Before Guy, Debs or I ever picked up a ball or bat, things were already in place for us to step into the sporting arena in one way or another. To begin with, I need look no further than my parents. Both had a huge interest in sport. My mum played hockey for Ireland. She played up front and was starting to put a string of caps together before marrying and moving across the water and setting up home in Yorkshire. In those days, travelling back and forth from England to Ireland to continue her sporting career would not have been an option, unlike later on, when Guy and I played rugby for Ireland. After moving to Yorkshire, she played hockey for Tadcaster. We used to go and watch her week in, week out as kids, and she would score goals for fun with three, four or five goals a game quite a common occurrence. She carried on playing until well into her forties. Guy and Debs picked up mum's interest in hockey, especially Debs, but I never took to it myself.

Dad was quite a handy boxer when he was young, keen on rugby and he played village cricket until after

I was born. He was one of those who got together to start a rugby team in Tadcaster. There had been a team in the town previously, formed way back at the end of the nineteenth century. It boasted a famous rugby son in those days. While playing for Tadcaster, William Bromet won his first cap for England in the 1891 Home Nations Championships, playing in a victory against Wales. He was a member of the first official British Isles tour abroad, the one that went to South Africa in 1891. He played in 19 out of the 20 games on tour, including the three Tests – two of which he played alongside his brother, Edward. William was an influential figure in the early days of rugby and was one of the eleven leading players who signed a public letter urging the clubs in the north of England not to go ahead with their plans to pay players for what was called 'broken time'. The eleven, who included the Barbarians' founder, William Percy Carpmael, were amateurs of conviction and strongly opposed any attempt to pay rugby players. This conflict among the clubs in the north eventually led to a split and the formation of rugby league in that part of the country in 1895.

Dad and a few others tried to bring the Tadcaster club back into being and succeeded in doing so for quite some time. But, by the time I came along, it had pretty much come to a halt again.

Saturdays for us kids were spent either watching mum play hockey or Guy and I going shooting with dad. I spent a good few years of my childhood either beating or loading for dad on shoots in the Yorkshire countryside. Shooting was a big passion for dad and it's been passed on to both my brother and I. He was a really good shot, as many people told me when I went on these shoots, but he was quite laid-back about his own shooting ability.

I remember going with him once, when I was about eight or nine, to a shoot a couple of hours away.

Dad shot the first drive but then he turned to me and said that I could shoot the second. I felt really proud that he'd asked me; it was a kind of rite of passage moment. It became obvious that more than the gun was passed to me as I ended up hitting eighteen out of the nineteen birds! At the end of the drive, people were making comments again about how good a shot *Henry* was.

"No, no, it wasn't me. That was Simon shooting!"

I won't forget the pleasure with which he said those words as he turned to his friends. I was beaming! There was a sense of being a chip off the old block, as I already knew how good others thought dad was. It was nice to be seen to keep up with him. It's also probably the best I've ever shot – which is not quite so good, maybe!

Living on such a large farm gave us ample opportunity to indulge other sporting activities as well. At home we would have a set of goalposts for football, an area set aside for place kicking, which dad would join us for, as well as a fifteen-yard by fifteen rugby pitch. There was an area for playing cricket, a makeshift part for playing tennis (as opposed to the grass tennis court which we didn't play on), and I even tried to cut out a golf green in the garden! So when I talk of this idyllic childhood, those sporting areas were its parameters.

Along with normal day-to-day farm life, this meant, of course, that we were in the great outdoors for most of our daylight hours. Every time we washed our hair, we weren't allowed to dry it indoors with a hairdryer or towel. It was a case of 'get out into the fresh air and let it dry naturally'! Television was restricted quite firmly and programmes such as *Grange Hill*, for example, were out of bounds. Mum thought that it would be a bad influence on us. So, when kids at school used to talk about the programmes they'd seen on TV the night before, I would restrict my comments to the trailers I'd seen earlier. I did feel a little left out by this, if I'm honest. But now, looking back, it did me no harm – as my mum keeps telling me to this day! It would have been difficult to watch a lot of television anyway because, until the time I was about ten years old, I was in bed each night by 6 p.m. Again, that is something my mum says did me no harm, as the three of us grew up to be fit and healthy people. Mum was quite strict and wanted us to be polite and well-mannered children – hence the TV deprivation!

I say that my mum was strict; one reason for this maybe is the fact that when I was two years old, my parents split up. It might seem strange that so far I've talked about this idyllic childhood, and now I mention a rather traumatic event in any family's life. And I'm sure it was, at the time, for all involved. But, our situation was different to most. Mum, Guy, Debs and I continued to live at Kirby Grange and dad was the one who moved out. But, because of the farm business, we saw dad every day of the week and the sporting weekends kept us together. The only real difference for us, therefore, was the time when we came in for the evening and got ready to go to bed. We had no family time, as such, as a family of five. Dad rarely put us to bed. Mum wanted as much involvement from dad as possible, and that certainly happened, giving me a stability that I might not otherwise have had; it saved me from any major emotional wrench. Debs and Guy were older than me and the break-up might have affected them in a different way, especially Debs, who was six years older than me. But, looking back, not one of the three of us can say that we were without the influence and guiding hand of both parents, even if they were apart.

Mum and dad, then, had this natural competitive sporting instinct. But as much as we were immersed in watching and playing sport, we also inherited a certain attitude towards sport. I appreciated how competent both my parents were at the sports they took up. As I would learn for myself at the top level of rugby, tactics and fitness are only two elements in a sportsman's game. The 'top two inches' are what makes the real difference. I reckon that I got a lot of that when I was a little boy playing on a Yorkshire farmyard.

3

The Doyles of Dublin

FROM THE MOMENT the first guns of the Second World War were fired, Ireland kept a position of complete neutrality refusing, under de Valera's leadership, to join either the Allies or Axis powers. But, despite this, for almost a year until the summer of 1941, many parts of the country were bombed by Hitler's planes, particularly the area surrounding Dublin. Dun Laoghaire was hit first, and then various areas of the capital over many nights in 1941. Between the rubble of both bomb-torn areas, lay the quiet semi-rural, semi-suburban village of An Charraig Dhubh, or Blackrock as it's known in English. Now it's a suburb of Dublin and it's in this area that my mum, Catherine, was born, not long after the German planes had left their mark on so-called neutral Ireland.

Mum's family were descended from farming stock as well, back to the generation of her grandparents. Both granny and granddad were the youngest of eleven and nine children, respectively. My grandmother's family were O'Mearas and came from a farming community in Tipperary. It's one of those strange twists that Tipperary was so large that it had to be divided into two Ridings, just as the Yorkshire my mother would live in. That part of Ireland also had a strong presence of English landowners, and a landed gentry tradition as a result. Granny's great great-grandfather would have to buy his land back from the British and this was the start of a tradition of the farm being passed on to the eldest son. When the farm passed on to my granny's elder brother, she chose to leave the farm and headed to Dublin. Incidentally, her eldest brother was awarded the MC in the First World War, fighting for the Munster Fusiliers.

My grandfather's family had their roots in the Wicklow/Dublin border country and he later moved to Dublin too. But, they weren't from a farming background. My great-grandfather was master of the South Dublin Union, a large complex of workhouse and hospital buildings on a site now shared by St James' Hospital and Trinity College in Dublin. This was the scene of some vicious fighting during the Easter Rising of 1916, when a nurse was killed.

My first experience of Ireland would have been fairly soon after I was born, as we went there every year for a holiday. Usually, we spent about four weeks there every summer and then another week at Christmas. Within a mile radius of where granny and granddad lived, there were plenty of other family members: great aunts, aunts, uncles and cousins. When in Dublin we would stay with granny and granddad at their home on Stradbrook Road, a house which had the wonderful name of Summer. That, actually, pretty much sums up my childhood experiences of Ireland.

We stayed mostly in and around Blackrock, spending a great deal of our time on the beaches of the area. I loved going to Sandycove, also to the Forty Foot which was, until recently, a male only bathing beach, and then across to White Rock near Dalkey. The occasional trip away from these places would take us down to Brittas Bay near Wicklow. It's an amazing beach and since the 1950s has been a very popular summer house location for Dubliners. Part of the film *The Count of Monte Cristo* was filmed on its sands about ten years ago. I enjoyed the vast expanse of open beach and its sweeping bay. We went to the east coast more than anywhere else in Ireland, and I loved every minute of it.

Staying for such a lengthy period every year made me really enjoy experiencing the Irish way of life. I think I appreciated it far more than if we'd stayed in Yorkshire or done the usual foreign package holiday every summer. Sometimes my mum's brother Eddie and his wife Evelyn would holiday with us, and that was great because they had four boys of their own, Gerard, Alan, Eric and Simon.

Not only was I surrounded by family when we were there, but we also got to know my grandparents' neighbours and other people in the area, as well as other children. Each year we would pick up the relationship with them where we'd left off. To me, Blackrock was like a city, even though it wasn't, of course. When mum was growing up there it was no more than a village. And it was so different from back home in Yorkshire; it might just as well have been a metropolis. I enjoyed that change very much. It was in stark contrast to the isolation we felt during summer days back home, when we'd hardly see a soul from day to day. On the farm, it was me, my brother and sister and my imaginary friends – but I'm not too sure if I want to mention them!

Added to the fun of being with so many people in Ireland was the opportunity to be totally spoiled by my grandmother. Not far from their house was an ice-cream parlour which she would let us go to on our own. That was great, although we probably wouldn't do it these days because, although it was close by, it was out of sight of their home. Ice-cream wafers were all the rage then, a thick block of ice-cream between two thin wafers, and we just had to indulge as often as we could. Granny, of course, would fund this indulgence!

Not such pleasant a memory is the one of the tinkers who used to be seen on the streets in Dublin. They frightened me quite a bit. They would go round on a horse and cart, something which I hadn't seen in Yorkshire at all. To be fair to the tinkers, I think my fear had a lot to do with my brother and sister who took great delight in telling their little brother that if I went near any of them, they would snatch me up and take me away! So for me, every tinker in Dublin was the child catcher in *Chitty Chitty Bang Bang*!

One person whom we visited regularly on our trips to Ireland was my Godfather Charles Lysaght. Myself and Charles shared a keen interest in cricket, Charles even playing against me at Ampleforth on a couple of occasions during our Exhibition weekends. Mum and Charles had grown up knowing one another as Charles' Auntie Moira was one of Granny's best friends. His father Charlie was also close to Granny and her family. Charles' father, who eventually became Chief Medical Adviser to the Department of Health in Ireland, was a medical student at the Mater Hospital in Dublin during the Irish War of Independence between 1919 and 1921. At this time of unrest, called the Troubles, he, along with other members of the hospital staff, would protect the injured members of the IRA, not necessarily because of any political allegiance but out of respect for doctor patient confidentiality. Mum trained as a physiotherapist in the Mater and loved hearing Charles' father's accounts of gunshot victims being admitted to the hospital during the Troubles and how the medics put down 'appendicitis' on their medical boards as the reason for admission, thereby concealing these injured IRA men when the Black and Tans searched the Hospital. The Black and Tans, who had been recruited mainly from British World War I veterans to boost the numbers of the Royal Irish Constabulary, had made themselves very unpopular for taking reprisals against the civilian population.

The Black and Tans' tactics among the civilian population of Dublin included making random visits to the homes of the city's residents, to look for any IRA members or sympathisers. During one such raid on homes, they got near my blood family as well. Granddad was the youngest of nine brothers and they lived at the time in the Phoenix Park area of Dublin, near Kilmainham Jail, where Michael Collins and other nationalists had been executed. One day, when granddad's parents were out at the Phoenix Races, their house, Garden Hill, was visited by the Black and Tans. When my grandparents returned from the races, they found soldiers brandishing guns and questioning the nanny, as well as some of the younger boys, including my granddad. They asked to be shown around the house, and then they saw a framed photograph of a family member in uniform. It was one of my mum's great uncles who had fought in the Boer War with many other Irishmen. On learning that he was an officer in the Buffs Regiment of the British Army, the Black and Tans left my family in peace. Their thinking was that with so many fit and active young men in one household, at least one of them would surely be an IRA member. If that was their logic in the Dublin of the time, they would have had their work cut out just going round to all the households with ten boys!

In our family, I'm fairly certain that none of the young men they were looking for were actually IRA members, although I would suspect that many had republican sympathies. One of those ten boys then went on to become aide-de-camp, or personal assistant, to the first President of Ireland, Douglas Hyde.

Some have questioned my Irish links, including one or two fellow Irish internationals, obviously offended by an Englishman wearing the green of Ireland. The first thing that quietens such suspicion is telling them that I consciously chose to play for Ireland, having already turned England down. That usually works. Then, if more persuasion is needed, I guess the family story I've just related here, speaks for itself.

4

The Easterbys of Yorkshire

AT ONE TIME, it was said that it was quicker and cheaper to get to Yorkshire from Ireland than from many other parts of England, such as Dorset or Norfolk, for example. Ireland-Yorkshire was a well-trodden route with cities such as Bradford having a huge Irish population well over 150 years ago. My grandfather, Papa, was one who made the journey from Yorkshire to Ireland as a young man, not far off a hundred years ago.

Walter Easterby was born in Hunslet, a farming area just outside Leeds in 1892. His dad, Henry, was a blacksmith who also ran a pub and owned land in the village of Deighton, near York. They then moved to Frodingham in the East Riding. The fact that Henry was a blacksmith is the first obvious connection between my family's long tradition with the world of horses. It's a link that's still strong. In his teens Papa whipped in the hunt with the West Carberry Hounds in Cork. Papa couldn't go to the front line during the First World War because he had glandular fever, but he did serve abroad behind the front line, tending to the horses which were such an integral part of the war effort. His brother Billy served with him and he was badly gassed during combat. They served in Lord Lindsey's Company and, at the end of the war Lord Lindsey asked Papa if he'd be willing to be his factor and horse trainer at his estate in Coupar, Scotland. He turned down the factor's job, but did train Lord Lindsey's horses. He then moved from Scotland back home to Yorkshire, where he continued to train horses, commencing at Middleham, an area where racehorses have been trained for over 200 years. He continued to train Lord Lindsey's horses there. It wasn't long before he achieved his first winner, Pure Scandal, which won in a race at Thirsk in 1933, a horse ridden by none other than the master himself, Gordon Richards.

Papa then moved on to Malton, where dad was born. He took his family to the Stockwell Stud, which had been in operation since the middle of the nineteenth century and a training stables during the twentieth century. It was originally known as Kirkby Farm, but was renamed to commemorate the great sire Stockwell, an amazing horse who was a seven-time champion sire, sire of three Derby winners, and the winner of the 2,000 Guineas and the St Leger. Papa also trained for Lord Fitzwilliam. Lord Fitzwilliam had wanted Papa to go to Wicklow to work as a trainer, but he remained in Yorkshire and set up the Rockingham Stud company with the Fitzwilliam family. The training turned into breeding and this is what my dad took up when his time came, although he was more of a farmer than a horse breeder.

Papa had a second in the Grand National with Melleray's Belle in 1930 and a third with Acthon Major in 1950. The photograph of this horse clearing Becher's Brook takes pride of place at home. When I was young this particular fence looked like a huge mountain and I remember Papa saying that the fences were as hard as stone in those days. He also trained a horse that won the Ayr Gold Cup.

He retired from training at Stockwell when dad took over the farm. A house was built for Papa and Nana about 150 metres from the farm, as well as one for dad's sister Davina and her husband Phil Cockroft. Phil and Davina have also been in the horse breeding business for a long time. In contrast to my dad, they are horse breeders rather than farmers. And all this coincided with mum and dad getting married and Debs being born in 1969.

Peter and Mick Easterby, my great uncle Billy's sons, were regulars at the Stockwell Stud in their late teens and moved to live with Papa so that they could learn their trade. The arrangement obviously worked well as they went on to train numerous winners. Peter trained many Cheltenham Festival winners in the late 1970s and early '80s, including Sea Pigeon, a Champion Hurdle winner twice, as was Night Nurse, who also came second in the Gold Cup to stable companion Little Owl in 1981. Peter's five Champion Hurdle victories are a record for the race (currently shared with Nicky Henderson). Mick also trained many winners, including Mr Snugfit, runner-up to Last Suspect in the 1985 Grand National, and on the flat won the Group One 1,000 Guineas at Newmarket with Mrs McArly in 1977. Tim, Peter's son is carrying on the family tradition as is David, Mick's son, ensuring yet another generation of Easterbys train and breed horses.

But to me of course, Walter Easterby was grandfather – not a top racehorse trainer with all the above achievements – just Papa. The first time I was really conscious that he might be a bit of a 'name' was on his ninetieth birthday. I was surprised that the outside world was paying so much attention to the occasion. I was about ten years old then, when *Racing Magazine*, I think, came to take photos of him and write a piece about him. I was intrigued to hear them ask him to do certain things, like mucking out, so that they could have a variety of photos. He loved all that and was certainly not publicity shy. I remember thinking that this didn't happen in normal family life. And then a picture started to form in my mind as I thought of all those framed photos on the walls, some showing the Queen presenting him with one trophy or another – that maybe Papa was something special to people other than me. Now of course, I fully appreciate his contribution to the horse racing world.

He worked on the farm well into old age and was a fit, hard worker. During the summer holidays, when us kids would enjoy a nice lie-in as often as we could, Papa would come up to the house and throw stones at the windows to wake us up! "Why the hell are these lads not up yet?" would be his constant cry, "they should be working!" He didn't stop doing this even when getting around proved to be more difficult in later years. Maybe dad shouldn't have bought him that mobility scooter!

He lived until he was 94 and there was a secret to his long life. He would drink half a bottle of Moët champagne every day and smoke a cigar – and that ritual took place not at the end of the day, but every morning! That's unusual enough anywhere, but really unusual considering he was a real, dyed-in-the-wool proud Yorkshireman. It was quite an experience to go down the lane to Papa's house and see this broad Yorkshireman with a stereotypical Yorkshire accent, with farming in his veins, sipping his Moët before lunch. It's an early memory for me, so he must have done it for years. I'm not going to argue with the indulgence, it evidently worked!

That ritual may hint at one side of Papa, the fun-loving guy who liked a good time. He made a very good living from his horse training and breeding, and this brought him into the aristocratic world of racehorse owners, with the lifestyle that involves. He worked hard for his money but, unfortunately, bad accounting advice cost him a considerable amount of that hard-earned cash.

Dad carried on Papa's work for a long time and had successes of his own as well. He had highly-rated stallions for quite a long time – Officio and Precocious being two of the better known. He kept his own horses too, as well as taking in the horses of other owners. If an owner wanted a brood mare covered, it would come to us and either stay for the duration of the pregnancy or go back to the owners for that period of time and sometimes back to us again for the birth. We usually had 60 to 70 horses at the stables at any given time, with obviously enough individual stables to take that number. Dad built the stable up to be one of high reputation and it employed 25 people, as well as the five he employed to work on the farm. But all this took its toll. He had to work hard for very little reward and worked himself to a standstill, as illnesses became more frequent. In the end, he decided to give it up as the rewards weren't there in proportion to the work needed to achieve them. The stables turned from breeding to livery and dad turned his attention more towards farming. But, whatever the nature of dad's business was, it all meant a hell of a lot of muckracking for Guy and me every school holiday! When I left secondary school I worked on the farm for a year, but by then dad had thankfully turned the farm more towards growing crops. EU subsidies meant a lot less muck for me!

Through a few accidents of history, Yorkshire and Ireland have intertwined in my family. No doubt that the love of horses and horse racing is a massive link between these two areas. This is certainly where I get my love of horse-racing from, even if my horse riding didn't go anywhere! Today, I co-own a racehorse called Ski Sunday with Welsh record cap holder Stephen Jones and former Scarlets chief executive, Stuart Gallagher, who is now one of the directors of European rugby. I had always wanted to own a horse, and in 2007 we paid over the odds for a horse at a sale. As it turned out Ski Sunday is a pretty good horse. We put him with the young enthusiastic trainer, Tim Vaughan, and in his first season he ran a second at Cheltenham and at Aintree. We had an amazing start to our racehorse owning careers!

But then, disaster struck and Ski Sunday lost an eye following an infection. After recovering, there followed a period of moving from trainer to trainer. Now he's back with Tim again, the person he's had the most success with. Ski Sunday has now moved on from hurdling to jumping over fences. Therefore, I carry on that part of my family tradition in my own way and I'm sure that Papa would be more than proud of me.

But there's more than the love of horses to link Ireland and Yorkshire for me. The connections between the two culminated, of course, with my dad meeting my mum.

My upbringing was a mix of two distinct geographical areas which had a strong sense of their own identity in the face of outside influences. Both the Ireland and the Yorkshire of my formative years felt the need to assert themselves as being different from anything British or English. I was definitely aware of living in Yorkshire, but not so much of living in England. I was also aware that being Irish was very different to being English.

5

Prayers and Black Eyes

THERE WAS A time when the phone would ring back home at Kirkby Grange and we'd hear Guy in floods of tears at the other end. He was at Ampleforth College in North Yorkshire, the largest boarding school of its kind in the United Kingdom. He was having a bit of a tough time there because he didn't fit in with the rest – the other kids considered him to come from a more rural background than they thought was acceptably cool. But, this only lasted for the first few months of Guy's time at Ampleforth and in a cruel kind of younger brother way, I would benefit from his misery when it was my turn came to go to the same school. He'd prepared the way for me; I knew what to expect and, although I had exactly the same kind of treatment, I was ready for it and had Guy's words of encouragement to keep me going.

To go to Ampleforth meant leaving my primary school a year earlier than my contemporaries and it meant moving up to the 'big school' when I was ten, not eleven. It was a wrench to leave my family home at such a young age, because my life up until that point had been so happy. But, it turned out to be the right move for us. Dad had been to a boarding school in Cumbria, much further away from his home than I would be from mine. When my mum was growing up in Dublin, she had friends who went to Ampleforth and she knew of its quality. Our upbringing had been Catholic and we went to Mass regularly – maybe not as regularly as we had to at Ampleforth, but we did go! So the principle of a boarding education was already well established in my family.

Because Guy was there ahead me, I had already visited the school to watch him play rugby or cricket. I was totally captivated by the wide open spaces, the endless rugby pitches – twenty-six in all! The cricket pitches – six of those and fifteen tennis courts, as well as a swimming pool, squash courts, the five-a-side soccer pitches, the golf course and everything else. This was heaven and much more than Guy and I had on the farm! Added to this was the huge attraction of being able to play on these pitches with boys of my own age and not have to play against my older brother all the time and get beaten, more often than not!

I had also been there with mum and dad to what was called the exhibition. This was held every May and it basically showcased all the pupils' work throughout the year, in various exhibition formats. The art work was displayed, the photography... any form of work in fact. There was also a cricket match between the first team and a touring men's club called the Yorkshire Gents. The whole weekend culminated with the headmaster's speech. All this enthralled me – I wanted to be a part of it and Guy's tears weren't going to put me off!

What a total contrast to the small village primary school I had attended! But when I got to Ampleforth, other things, on a deeper level, started to become apparent. There was no hiding place in my primary school, but at Ampleforth, if you didn't get totally involved in the school's life, then kids could get isolated quite quickly, especially in the first couple of years. This was especially true for the foreign pupils who came from so far away, some from the USA and the Far East, and into *such* a different environment. Fitting in was even harder for them and some found it very difficult.

I found it tough at the beginning too. I was in a Yorkshire school, an hour from home, with a Yorkshire accent, yet I probably fitted in the least and I certainly felt as if I was in a minority. I was getting verbal abuse in a school in Yorkshire because I came from Yorkshire! It was a complete about-face from the primary school where we were all Yorkshire kids.

My first impressions, therefore, were somewhere between surreal and strange. There was no obvious reason for it to be so, but I had that strong feeling of being an outsider. And that was a feeling that would come back to haunt me in international dressing rooms in years to come.

So, in 1985, I started at Ampleforth, a boys' school run by the Benedictine monks of Ampleforth Abbey, about two miles from the village of Ampleforth on the southern edge of the North Yorkshire Moors National Park. The school had been opened in 1802, at the height of the Napoleonic War when a small group of men arrived at Ampleforth Lodge, fresh from the experience of being thrown out of a similar establishment in Lancashire. At Ampleforth, they set about establishing what was left of their monastic life.

Today, there are 81 monks there, although only about twelve are directly involved with the teaching. So I wasn't just going to a boys-only school, but into an ancient monastic community with a way of life that had been in place for nearly two centuries. Old boys included Andrew Parker Bowles, Lawrence Dallaglio, Radio 4's Edward Stourton, the former Tory MP Michael Ancram and the actor Rupert Everett.

There were three school years in the junior house which, when I started there, had about 150 boys. Father Henry was my housemaster. At thirteen years of age it was up to the upper school, which had ten houses, all named after saints. I was in St Hugh's, which is where Guy was also. Each housemaster was a monk and led the daily prayers. But nothing was as much of a rude awakening as having to do both Latin and Greek as part of my timetable! What a shock for a ten year-old! Thank goodness one of the boys had a remote controlled car which entertained us no end and he managed not to get it confiscated. The car would be let loose around the Latin classroom and the teacher would chase it around the desk with no idea whose it was! Us boys found it absolutely hysterical. After a year of studying these ancient languages it was decided that I would be doing classical studies in year two – basically the option you had to take if you were really bad at the two languages! Classical studies still involved learning about the Roman and Greek worlds, but only the history and culture, not the languages, thank goodness.

It was a structured, disciplined life at Ampleforth and the school week ran something like this. The school day would start with prayers at 7.30 a.m. for about ten to fifteen minutes and then breakfast, which was really good usually. We were then expected to be at our desks in the classroom by 8.45 a.m. for the first of five morning lessons. There was an added facet to this routine also: an early morning cross-country run of about four miles, which we had to do before prayers. Quite often we would leave in the dark at about 5 a.m. to make sure we got back by 7.30 a.m. The teachers weren't daft either. To make sure we actually did the run, we had to post a letter in a certain place near the lake in the school grounds and a teacher would go there during the day to collect the letters.

Once the lessons had begun there was no option to go back to your dormitory if you had a free lesson – that luxury was only offered to the sixth form. We had to stay in the school building, where we each had a carrel desk of our own to keep our books. Once the five morning lessons were over, we would head for our carrels for a prep period, between 12.30 and 1 p.m. Then, it was back up to our house for food, before going on to the sports fields on Tuesdays, Wednesdays and Fridays from 2 p.m. until about 3.30 p.m., then tea and back to class for three lessons until 6 p.m. More prep time afterwards, supper an hour later, and then back up to our house. There was some free time at about 8 p.m. which we would spend playing cricket or five-a-side football, unless we went up to the lounge to watch some telly. The day ended with prayers again at 9.30 p.m. Thursday nights were different, because that's when we had our weekly house Mass, again taken by the monks. Every house had its own chapel. It was very structured and we managed to cram a great deal into every day. As soon as prayers were over, especially in the first three years, we were really tired and ready for bed – which was so much later of course than the time my mum used to put me to bed back home!

Monday and Thursday afternoons gave us a chance to do something other than rugby. Every Monday afternoon was given over to activities linked with one of the armed forces: either army, navy or air force cadets' activities. I chose what was considered to be the easiest of the options, the army! These afternoons were actually quite fun and we would do loads of different things, such as orienteering, marching, or going away to various camps – all fully kitted-out in our army uniform. Using the indoor shooting range was great for me, as it took me back to the shooting I had done with dad on the various hunts. The targets at Ampleforth weren't moving targets unfortunately, so it wasn't quite as challenging, but it kept my eye in.

Break time every morning wasn't a break at all. All those playing for either the A or B teams of any age – under-14s, 15s, 16s, and the first teams – headed straight to the old-fashioned gym with its hard wooden floors and bars on each wall. This is where some extra rugby work was done, concentrating on set pieces such as the scrum and the line-outs. This might come as a bit of a surprise to most, especially my fellow international forwards, but at that time I played hooker for the school. Yes, it could well have been a case of move over Keith Wood! So, as a first choice hooker, the break times were particularly busy for me, practising my line-out throws and my scrummaging. There was nothing like twenty minutes of scrummaging for sending you back to your lessons dripping in sweat and smelling to high heaven!

Thursday afternoons gave us another opportunity for a sporting session, if that's what we chose to do. We could play any of the sports not considered to be a core sport, sports such as swimming or five-a-side soccer. Alternatively, we could go to the arts centre. I tended to do a bit of both because, when I got to Ampleforth, I realised that I had an interest in photography. I ended up doing it for GCSE and A Level, earning an A grade in both. And if seeing the exhibition when I visited the school before becoming an Ampleforth pupil filled me with awe, imagine the feeling when I saw my own work exhibited at that prestigious annual event for everyone to see. The hours spent with my photography, especially in the dark room developing my work, were such a total departure from knocking my head against a gym wall! Landscape and architectural photography was what I really enjoyed doing and I loved the whole creative process, from taking the picture through to holding the print in my hand. Rugby has obviously taken over since then, but it would be great to go back to taking photos at some stage.

So, that was the structure of my school life for eight years. It was highly organised but gave me so many opportunities. Yes, it took a while to get used to being away from home, but that faded after a few months. I always felt that the boys who were day pupils missed out on so much in having to go home at about 6 p.m.

Ampleforth gave me a rugby grounding more than anything else. By the very fact that there were twenty-six rugby pitches, it was obvious that this was a rugby school. Quite simply, rugby was compulsory. We never played football against any other schools, but three or four teams in every year group would turn out regularly to play rugby against other schools. Our main rivals were Sedbergh in Cumbria, another boarding school.

They had a very well-known old boy who was doing quite well for England at the time I was starting senior school, the England captain, Will Carling. That gave the boys at his old school a definite lift and he was a huge source of inspiration. The senior years would put out seven teams against each other for that fixture, with the other years fielding four teams each. What a buzz that created whether we played at home or away! When we travelled, it was a case of a whole fleet of coaches and minibuses heading north on the three or four-hour journey, and if we were at home, we would be welcoming a whole convoy of vehicles. They were fantastic occasions.

In my case, Sedbergh is the first place where I played team rugby. In those first few years I played Number 8, probably because I was larger than most of the boys. I was still quite big for my age at ten, but maybe a bit more 'tank' than 'podge' by then! But as I grew older, the other boys caught up with me and I was no longer needed at Number 8 – I think my lack of pace kicked-in then as well! Then came the change to hooker, a position I played at until my very last year in school, when I went back to being a Number 8. I actually never played flanker throughout my whole time at Ampleforth – that was a later development.

Early on I was given the captaincy which, if nothing else, proved that I had skills on the rugby pitch even if I didn't have any academic ones! It was always a close call between me and a really gifted outside-half, George Hickman, to be the captain, and that was the case pretty much throughout school. We were both quite competitive in everything we did. George had really quick feet and, looking back, was a player who was very much in the Phil Bennett mould. The team was built around George and me, with my build and his skill being the focus of the team.

Another future England international, Lawrence Dallaglio, was at the school when I started there too. He was in the sixth form when I was in my first year, and he was a school year below Guy. My brother played in the same team as him, the second team, as Lawrence – or Del Boy as he was known in school – never played for the first team at Ampleforth. At that time, the firsts remained unbeaten for three seasons, and getting into the firsts was extremely difficult – not even a future World Cup winner could get in then! He excelled at rugby sevens then and the only other things I can remember about him is that he was a huge bloke and a bit of a rebel. He shared the same first name as the founder of the abbey, but this Lawrence was no saint! Inadvertently he would play a central role in my career in years to come, but more of that later.

Those all-conquering first teams had a huge influence on us younger boys. We held them all in high esteem. When we finished our games, we would run across to the firsts pitch, the match ground, to watch the end of their games and learn so much from the last ten minutes of play. But the astounding thing about those three unbeaten teams is that no individual player ever went on to make a mark for himself in first-class rugby after leaving the school. I sometimes wonder if they all had the rugby success they could take during that period, and anything else, later, would have been overkill. Or maybe, it was a case of it being a team effort for three years, with the Ampleforth spirit being the unifying factor, and when they left the school that enthusiasm for success on the rugby pitch disappeared.

I had my first taste of sporting disappointment at Ampleforth too. As I said, I was captain from really early on and all the talk was that I would be the firsts team captain in the sixth form. But that didn't happen. When I got to the upper sixth, the captaincy was either going to be given to me or a guy called James Hughes. He was selected, not me. The firsts team coach was John Wilcox, an ex-England international and British Lion. He was also the housemaster of St Cuthbert's, James Hughes' house. To me, at the time, it was rather obvious why James had been chosen and not me! Not getting the captaincy was quite a body blow for me, having gone through the whole school in that position of leadership on the field, only to fail and get the 'big one' in my final year. But now, looking back, that decision did me no harm. Jim had obvious leadership qualities; he later became a major in the army. John Wilcox taught me and many other young rugby players how to play the game in the right way, how to respect opponents but, at the same time, have the will to beat them fair and square. Maybe some players I've come up against throughout my career would question whether I was one of John Wilcox's successes, in that respect!

6

Faith and Failings

FOR OVER TEN years I've lived in a land where rugby is a religion. As all-pervasive as rugby was at Ampleforth, it was also very clear that rugby came second to religion, at least in the way school life was run. The daily prayers to begin and end every day, the weekly Mass in our house, were all deliberately structured to be the pillars of our time there.

But, without doubt, the main religious event of the week was the Sunday Mass. This was held in the abbey, a huge, imposing building to look at from the outside, but very light and simple inside. Mass was scheduled at 10 a.m. every Sunday which, if nothing else, meant we always had a lie-in. It was a really big event, and Catholics from the surrounding area would come to the abbey on Sundays, as would our families and friends if they wanted to. There was quite a lot of pomp to the service, with a full choir, fifty to sixty ordained monks and all the rituals and routines of a high Catholic Mass. It was quite special. After the service, we were allowed to go to local pubs or restaurants for Sunday lunch with our families. It was regarded as a day of rest.

A big factor in determining exactly how Sunday went was what we did on a Saturday night. Staying away from Mass wasn't an option. But when it came to going out for Sunday lunch or not, it was either a case of politely declining (because you just wanted to nurse your hangover), or it was a matter of going out with a hair of the dog attitude! For all its strictness and formality, Ampleforth was in many ways a very liberal school. We didn't have a school uniform, for example. But, there was a strict dress code of trousers, jacket, shirt and tie. Some housemasters relaxed this rule even, and some of the older boys could be seen walking around campus wearing ripped jeans and paisley shirts.

Normally, on Saturdays, we would have lessons in the morning and then, if we didn't play any team sport, we would be free until supper at about seven. In the sixth form however, there was another 'arrangement'. By 12.30 p.m. every Saturday, the local pubs within a six or seven-mile radius of the school would be full of Ampleforth boys. I'm sure that the powers that be in the school had an agreement with the landlords so that this could happen. The rumour has it that they justified this by saying that you could have two pints if you bought a meal. We were supposed to stay there for a couple of hours but it was usually about 5 or 6 p.m. by the time some left. Many pupils would walk a mile or two to the pub and walk back; others would take a taxi and go a little further away, with some venturing as far as York, twenty miles away.

Once we went to this pub about 15 minutes taxi ride away. By the time we'd finished pouring in, way after closing time, there must have been about seventy of us in there – much to the landlord's delight, of course. But in the days prior to texting, there was no sure way of knowing if there was going to be a police raid or not. A rumour was started that the police were on their way. We all left either through the kitchen, over the bar, or through every possible exit hole and ran as fast as we could. One lad and I left through a window and ran into the woods just as some of the monks arrived, with one or two policemen in tow for back-up. We had already called a taxi before our tip-off and, as we ran through the fields, we met it on the road coming towards us. It stopped, we jumped in and drove right past the outside of the pub, past all the lads who had been caught by the monks and the police! We took great delight in watching them all being rounded up and marched back to school as we sat in the back of the taxi!

People in the local communities didn't seem to object either, probably because the school employed many local people, especially on the farm it owned. We were familiar with many of those living in the surrounding villages.

The strange thing is that incidents such as this happened fairly frequently but the college authorities never put a stop to our visits to the pub on a Saturday afternoon. It was a nice way of giving us some responsibility and freedom, and I think that's why it continued. But like all good things, it was misused by some. Thank goodness that the monks didn't allow those who wrongly took advantage of the system to rule the day; they stuck to their original convictions.

After I left the school, I learned that one or two of the monks had also abused their privileges, but in a far more serious manner. Two monks were convicted for indecent assaults on underage boys; another was given community punishment for a sexual assault on a sleeping 13-year-old boy. A fourth was asked to leave the monastic community in 2002 after admitting 'improper physical conduct' with a sixth former. Other cases have been mentioned too, with the press reporting that six Ampleforth monks were paedophiles, with up to 40 boys having been abused over a long period of time according to the police. All these offences came to light about ten years ago, and had occurred years earlier, some as far back as 1960.

The fourth monk mentioned above was my housemaster at one time and he offended against someone in my brother's year. I was never aware that any of this was happening when I was a pupil there, nor did I have any idea that the Father I knew was involved in anything untoward. While I was at the school I was wary of him and never actually got on with him, and neither did Guy. But I didn't put that down to any possibility of an unhealthy interest in me. He was just someone to avoid unless you really had to deal with him on some school matter or other. He was one of the few monks who certainly enjoyed the trappings of boarding school life. For example, he would be taken skiing a couple of times a year by the parents of some of the boys or on holidays to Malta with another family. He enjoyed the good life and the benefits that came with being a housemaster at Ampleforth.

The question that all these cases raised however, was, what role did the school authorities play in dealing with the abuse. The police have since seriously questioned the decision to deal with the whole matter internally. Some parents expressed their concerns about possible abuse to the Abbot at the time, Basil Hume, who later became the leader of the Catholic Church in the United Kingdom. He listened to the concerns but decided to deal with it internally within the school. The police have consistently claimed that other cases were allowed to happen because of that decision. I don't know whether that's true or not, but there's no doubt that these incidents at Ampleforth took place in the bigger catalogue of abuse scandals that rocked the Catholic Church in recent years, both in the UK and in Ireland. Apart from the obvious reaction that these deeds were despicable and wrong, it saddens me that it happened at a school which I attended and that one person I knew was involved.

But that hasn't diminished my enjoyment of school days at Ampleforth, and my appreciation of the education it gave me. Neither has it made me dismiss the entire Catholic faith because of a minority who completely misused their position of trust and committed such horrible offences. What I experienced at Ampleforth was a solid faith-based education. I can't pretend that I didn't whinge fairly often when it was time to go to prayers or Mass – quite often they did get in the way of far more important things like rugby, or if they didn't, they were just boring and a pain to go to!

But I can say that I've seen the important value of faith from my time at Ampleforth. It amazes me that ordained priests and monks can give their life over to what they believe in to such a degree. Like many of the boys I knew at Ampleforth, I haven't carried on practising my faith as devoutly as we did when at school. This is where the rugby and religion are similar in the Ampleforth context, it seems.

We've started to take our children, Soffia and Ffredi, to the Sunday school in a Welsh chapel. I think it's

My christening in 1975 with mum, dad, Debs, Guy, and great aunt Pauline

Debs, Guy and me on Dandy – poor, poor horse!

I must've been a busy child – I even wore a hard riding hat to protect me from myself!

Kirkby Grange, my childhood home

On a family holiday in Portugal in 1977
– surprise, surprise I'm eating again!

In our garden – the future
Fred Truman and Geoff Boycott!

Around the farm in a snowy winter
– but nobody told Guy that there
weren't any mountains in Yorkshire!

One of our
many Labradors
– Seamus with Guy
and me in 1982

Guy and me swimming in a freezing Sandy Cove, Blackrock – it was good for us, apparently!

"Can someone hurry up and take the photo… I need the toilet!"

At Summer, the home of my grandparents in Blackrock, with my cousins Gerard, Eric, Alan and Simon in 1987

Playing in 1986 at Ampleforth where my love for the game of rugby began

First XV rugby team at Ampleforth in 1993 – I didn't become the captain, but good times, nevertheless!

First XI cricket in 1992 – seriously, what are those outfits about?

Living the dream: my first professional contract playing for Leeds in November 1997

"OK – which one of you idiots has the ring?!"

A proud father of the bride – Elgan looks on as we take our vows

At last…
Mr and Mrs Easterby

My mum and dad proud to welcome the new Mrs Easterby

Me and my beautiful big sis on my wedding day

All beaming: Sarra, me and her parents Elgan and Kathryn

Debs, her husband Chris and my lovely niece Francesca, with Guy and his girlfriend Laurie

Sharing a moment during my wedding day with the great man

Sarra's glamorous mam-gu, Marianne

My ushers and best men – they scrubbed up well… considering!

Matt Cardey, Stephen Jones and Guy – my best men laughing at me, not with me, during my wedding speech!

What is he going to say next? Guy taking his opportunity to rip into his little brother on his wedding day!

The picture that was on the front page of the *Wales on Sunday* newspaper

© Huw Evans Agency

Honeymoon – Sarra on top of the world after spending the evening with Dominico Dolce… and me of course!

At a post-match function in Rome – Sarra flew out for less than 24-hours to watch me play and celebrate afterwards!

Comparing tummies! Only one winner there – Sarra 7 months pregnant with Soffia in December 2006

The first time I held Soffia; here she is at a few minutes old on 25 February 2007

Me and my little surfer chick in Dubai in December 2008

Born at 10lb 15oz on 1 May 2009, Ffredi was heavy even with my big guns!

Ffredi at a few minutes old but already looking like a three month old!

My three beauties – the day after bringing Ffredi home from hospital in May 2009

One of my favourite pictures of the four of us, with Ffredi just a few weeks old in May 2009

Our annual visit to see Siôn Corn (Father Christmas) in Harrods, London

"Yeah, thanks Dadi, the snowman's great… can we go in now please… I'm freezing!"

A fashionista on the tennis court in Cyprus in 2009

Ffred's rocking the suit and tie look!

Soffia – wise beyond her years

Like father like son!

Cwtch… squeeeeezzzz

The Rees Easterby gang star struck after meeting the one and only Buzz Lightyear at Disney World, Florida in June 2011

Our beautiful
babies in Naples,
June 2011

My bestest girl,
Soffia in Naples

Our little man with
his favourite food
– such a character!

The only girl in my house that doesn't answer me back! Our dog Darcy

All dressed up for a friend's 40th birthday in June 2011. It was a Disney theme, so Sarra was a modern Queen of Hearts and this is my take on the Mad Hatter (Johnny Depp style) from *Alice in Wonderland*!

We live a stone's throw from the beach and spend a lot of time there, come rain or shine

A lazy Sunday afternoon mowing the lawn

Ffredi after raiding my kit bags again!

Anyone seen Sarra?!

Surf's up, dudes – on one of
our visits to Cyprus

On a family holiday in America
– June 2011

Cousins Soffia, Ffredi, Francesca, Sebastian and Toby

Sebastian, sister Charlotte, Toby and Francesca

Our horse Ski Sunday – he's brought us a lot of joy over the years – but a special moment was watching the great A P McCoy ride him to victory at Kempton 2011

Soffia's first horse ride at home in Yorkshire

important for my children to have such a grounding. I believe that there is only one God, but He can be found in the Catholic Church, in Welsh chapels and in so many other places too. I have no desire to convert people to one type of faith and, similarly, no desire to persuade people who have faith that they shouldn't have it. Neither the scandals nor the strict religious regime at Ampleforth have made me rebel against the faith of my upbringing, even if I don't exercise that faith as often as I have done.

7

Aborigines, the Barmy Army and a Mail Room

IT WAS THE year of O J Simpson's famous cop car chase, the film *Schindler's List*, uncovering Fred West's atrocities, Brazil winning the football World Cup and Schumacher winning his first Formula One race. I left the comfortable world of Yorkshire to head down under. In 1994, it was time to spread my wings.

I didn't know a single soul when I arrived in Sydney. I had nowhere to stay, no job and no idea where to start. But I was determined it was going to work, so it was just a case of getting on with it and seeing what happened. I always knew that when I left Ampleforth I would go to Australia for a while to travel around and explore that fantastic country. Guy had done so when he left school and I wanted to follow his example. It didn't happen straight away and in the first year after leaving Ampleforth, I was back working on the farm and playing rugby for Harrogate.

Contacts are handy things and, as luck would have it, someone at Harrogate Rugby Club helped me out with my trip to Australia. Roger Shackleton, a former England fly-half, knew none other than Australian scrum-half legend Nick Farr-Jones, the 63-times capped Wallaby, whose club was Sydney University. I contacted Nick by letter, as one did in those days, and he was really helpful. He gave me the name and contact details of another Australian star, Dave Brockhoff. He was regarded as one of the greats of the game down under, having played for the Wallabies from 1949 to 1951. He'd then coached the Wallabies from 1974 to 1979. He had been heavily involved with Sydney University's rugby team also, and that's why I wanted to get in touch with him. I rang him as soon as I touched down on Australian soil and he was really welcoming and helpful. He asked me to contact him again when the Australian rugby season started and he would see what he could do to help me then. That was really encouraging. I arrived in Sydney in November '94 and their season would start in April '95.

So, I had plenty of time on my hands before thinking about playing any rugby and I had a huge continent to explore. Look out Australia!

My time in Oz didn't exactly get off to a flying start though. I arrived at Sydney airport after a 24-hour flight with nothing but a backpack. No arrangements had been made – and a place to sleep was the first thing to be sorted out. The general plan was to find work and do some travelling. I caught a bus to the King's Cross area of the city. The Cross, as it's known locally, is basically the red-light district and the most densely populated part of Australia with over 20,000 people crammed into less than a square mile. I certainly had a vibrant welcome as I walked off the bus into the glare of the massive neon Coca Cola sign and the buzz of hordes of people on the streets. But, I was there not for the red lights but to find a bed as it is the backpackers' HQ as well, where cheap accommodation could be found.

The next task was to find work. The hostels had plenty of ads on the noticeboards telling you about available jobs. I got a bar job in the Test Tube, one of the many strip-joints in The Cross. But glamorous it was not! My job was to wash the test tubes and the glasses and whatever else they used there. I left that job after a couple of days because it was, basically, shocking! In stark contrast, I then got a job with a removal firm. There were four or five of us backpackers to every removal van and the guy in charge was an Aussie. That job was OK. It was good money, we got to travel round the city a bit and all that lifting gave me a chance to stay fit as well. This job lasted a couple of months. Then it was back to the noticeboard to see what other jobs were available. My next job was packing CDs in a factory. Monotonous production line work and night-time work as well. It was supposed to be a couple of weeks worth of work and ten of us got jobs there. On our first shift we finished at six in the morning and the plan was to go back to the hostel for some sleep and then some free time before going back for the next shift later on that evening. But, as soon as we left the factory, we hit one bar after the other and on and on until one in the afternoon, and then, of course, slept through! Needless to say we didn't make the next shift or any other!

I really struck lucky when I bumped into four guys from Newcastle University who had taken a gap year after graduating. I ended up moving from my hostel to where they were staying. One day, the chat soon came round to what they really wanted to do – travel as far across Australia as was possible. That was my intention too, so we agreed we would all do it together.

We pooled the money we'd saved since arriving in the country, about A$2,500, and bought a blue Ford Falcon station wagon. So, at the beginning of February 1995, I hit the open Australian roads with the other four lads. New South Wales came and went, then Victoria, South Australia and into Western Australia. Ten days of driving for as long as we could in the daylight hours (as we'd been warned not to drive after dark because of the dangers of hitting kangaroos and camels – dangerous for them and our vehicles!).

It was rather obvious at times that we were novices abroad, and no more so than when we turned up at a beautiful beach which we'd been told had the best surfing. Five young lads strolled onto this beach with our boogie boards, ready for the action. Until, that is, we saw these guys strolling out of the water, wearing helmets, with cuts and bruises on their bodies and professional surf boards under their arms. We cleverly averted our path to the sea and lay down on the sand for a few hours watching the real surfers tackle the waves; the reef that was not that far under the surface of the water and there was also the threat of the great white sharks a little further out! Sunbathing was a lot safer!

This certainly was the real Australia. We stayed in hostels some nights but at other times we did just what had to be done and camped out under the stars. That was really quite something. Lying under the night sky with a few beers was quite an experience which was occasionally aided by experimenting with a few substances! But usually we didn't need these to appreciate the vast expanse of the open outback that we were part of night after night.

We did the touristy bit too. Just as we left New South Wales, we hit the town of Broken Hill, an isolated mining city in the outback of the state. It's a small city, with houses of corrugated iron sheets, where mining is still a way of life. Despite its remoteness – the closest major city is Adelaide, 300 miles away – the area has been used a lot as a film set. We managed to find the location used in the *Mad Max* film as well as the Foster's advert when the guy gets the fright of his life from a massive spider while sitting on the toilet! We didn't see the area they used in *Priscilla, Queen of the Desert*, though.

Broken Hill is typical of so many towns and cities in Australia. Broken Hill had an Aboriginal name originally, before it was changed in the nineteenth century to an English name. Up until then it was called Leaping Crest, which is slightly more imaginative than calling it Broken Hill, because it looked as if there was a break in the hills! We did come across the Aboriginal culture too on our travels and I must say it was a mixture of the delightful and the not so pleasant.

On the long stretches of open roads, there are what the Aussies call road houses, similar to our motorway service stations. Round the back of many of these, groups of Aborigines would gather for a smoke and a drink. Quite often we joined them and had a great time chatting. They were lovely people, polite and generous, with a sense of history and culture which I found fascinating. During my year in Australia, the government, for the first time, officially apologised for the displacement of Aborigines throughout the 1950s and '60s during the Maralinga nuclear tests. Attitudes were changing towards them without a doubt, but there were times when it was, to be honest, not difficult to see why some Aborigines attracted some negative reaction.

When we hit Perth, we saw a different side to some of them. They were now Aborigines in a big city, and this was not their natural environment. They were also Aborigines in a city where there was plenty of alcohol and that made a huge difference to their lives. Free from the restraint and guidance of their own communities, they hit the bottle, big time. It was quite common to see large groups of them with a bottle each, congregating in the parks. It was an encounter with one of these groups that gave me the biggest fright of my Australian trip. The hostel where we stayed at in Perth had a park across the road and a bottle shop, or off-licence to us, attached to it. They would walk across from the park to the shop quite often, but never safely, because they were drunk. One day, as we were standing by the roadside, we heard a loud screech, a thud and the sound of glass smashing as bottles broke. An Asian guy had driven down the road and had knocked one of the Aborigines over. It would have been very difficult for him not to, in fact.

All hell broke loose, and about twenty Aborigines wanted the blood of the Asian car driver who had knocked over one of their own. It was scary. We didn't want to get involved but we didn't want to see this guy come to any harm either. So we tried to rescue him as best we could. We dragged him away from the group of Aborigines, but not before we'd taken a few knocks and kicks to the head ourselves. Luckily, the bottle shop owner had seen all this and had called the police. They turned up pretty quickly, thank goodness.

There were plenty of homeless Australians in

the parks of Perth too, but they didn't seem to be as uncontrollably drunk as the Aborigines. That puzzled me. I was told that one possible reason was that the Aborigines had lived in the land we now call Australia for centuries before Westerners colonised it and subsequently introduced alcohol. That, so say some, means that they are not genetically predisposed to take alcohol. I don't know if that is true, but it certainly explains why two different groups of people, in the same circumstances, react totally differently to the same drink.

The whole incident was a massive wake-up call for me on a trip that was, to be honest, one long wake-up call. I had been pretty isolated and sheltered in Ampleforth. Getting caught in the pub after closing was about the height of any adventure which might have involved the police. But this was different. I had to grow up quickly and incidents like this one in Perth were a huge part of that.

But, just before I get too self-righteous, our time in Perth might well have left the Aborigines with a definite theory as to how the British behave while drinking as well! We still had some of the money that we'd all saved in Sydney, but we now wanted to find some work in Perth before thinking about the return journey. That didn't work out, unfortunately, which meant no income but a lot of time on our hands. That was lethal! Suffice to say that we pretty much ran amok in Perth and created quite a stir in the backpacking community.

And getting involved with the Barmy Army didn't help much on that front. England were over in Australia for a cricket Test series and we decided to watch the Perth match, which was the last of the five Tests. England had already lost the series, but that wasn't a consideration

– we were going anyway. It was the early days of the travelling England fans being called the Barmy Army, and we decided to get stuck in as well. Since those days, there's been a special place for the Australian cricketers and their fans in the Barmy Army banter. Their own website explains why, '… because there's nothing we like more than winding up the convicts'! So, it was great to be there in the early days, the five of us dressing up for the occasion in some silly costume or other. At that time there were about forty of us giving our own brand of support. These days, the Barmy Army can have up to 1,000 at a Test match. It was five days of non-stop drinking basically. The cricket wasn't bad either, with the likes of Michael Slater, Shane Warne, the Waugh brothers and Glenn McGrath from the Aussie team facing Michael Atherton's England which included Gatting, Gooch and Ramprakash. Despite Graham Thorpe's century, England lost this one too. But, as one of the early Barmy Army recruits, a good time was had by all!

So, between one thing and another, by the time we left the city, the talk was that we had been run out of town by men in white coats! Not sure if that was the case, but we definitely out-stayed our welcome. Just as well, as it was time to think about heading back to Sydney anyway, as the rugby season was about to begin and I had a phone call to make to Dave Brockhoff.

My Geordie friends were going further up to northern Australia, so I was going back on my own. I didn't fancy the long, arduous bus ride, so I scraped enough money together to pay for a flight back, about A$190. I had A$210 in my pocket, so I had some cash to spare as well!

Dave Brockhoff, true to his word from our first conversation, put me in touch with a few key people in the Sydney University rugby team and, once I was settled back into another hostel, I contacted them. One was the first team coach, Jim McInnerney, and the other, the backs' coach, Peter Farr-Jones, Nick's brother. I met them both at the university and they were fantastic. Not only were they keen for me to train with the team, but they also helped me find employment. The club captain, Martin Hide, was a student but he also worked in a pub in The Rocks. They got me a job there as well. This area, surrounded by water, is where they say the city originated. It's quite a touristy area but also has a lot of locals living and working there. The pub where Martin worked, the Palisade Hotel, was traditionally a local for the dockers, and it was just off the main tourist path. The pay was good and, more to the point, they gave me decent shifts which meant that I could concentrate on the rugby without work getting in the way. It wasn't another night-shift job packing CDs, thank goodness!

I went out to buy rugby boots, not having taken any with me, and my wallet, which contained all the money I had, was nicked. This forced me to do something I'd vowed not to do and had managed not to do for almost six months – phone home for cash! It really pained me to do so, especially having to reverse the charges of the phone call. It was a difficult time anyway: with very little cash I lived on supermarket own-brand cereal for every meal, scrounging milk from other hostel mates. I did this for two weeks, which was no good for me in any way. I hadn't started training with the club, and was trying to keep myself fit ready to join them, which was not easy on a diet like that.

Thank goodness everything kicked into place soon after that and I was training once again. The pub job was always going to be a stop-gap and later the university found me a job in the internal mail room. On my first day I thought that they had really stitched me up. Fifty or sixty bags of mail were waiting for me when I walked in, as there had been a postal strike and this was the backlog. Once I got over that shock however, it was a fantastic job. It was on campus and could fit around the training needs of the squad. What more could I ask for? On top of all that, I could enjoy university life, without the studies!

Sydney University is Australia's oldest and is very much along the lines of Oxford and Cambridge. It also has a rugby team of high regard. After some pre-season trials, I got into the team as a Number 8, and played for the under-20s, the Colts as they were called. That season turned out to be a really good one. We got to the Premier Rugby Grand Final that year, but lost out to Randwick, one of Australia's leading clubs, who had produced such legends as Ken Catchpole and the inimitable David Campese. It was an honour being able to play in the final of such a prestigious competition during my year in Australia. It couldn't have worked out better – well, it could have if we'd won of course!

I moved into a house with some of the other lads fairly soon. With a job sorted, my place in Sydney University's rugby team and living accommodation arranged, I really did settle in Australia and it became home for a good few months. I'd left the hostel scene, the string of temporary jobs and life was now what I would definitely call normal. I was now a guy who lived and worked in Sydney, and played rugby for a local team.

The university had five levels of teams, five 'grades' as they were called. But it wasn't that straightforward either. The fifth team would start match day, which was a Wednesday, and then each team would follow, culminating in the firsts being the last to play their game in the afternoon. But, everyone stayed around to watch the matches they weren't involved in. This led to a great sense of camaraderie, as we'd all cheer each other on, or chat over the barbecues that were running all day. Also, many players would take part in their own games and then be available as back-up for some of the other matches; they would then play more than one game in a day. That was something different again and was a good way of linking teams to each other and creating a definite structure of development as well. And the socialising would continue as only the Aussies know how.

Without knowing it at the time, Sydney University's rugby club gave me a strong taste of what was to come in the rugby world generally. They were still amateur days, but Sydney University's team were moving into the professional era, not by paying their players, but in trying to attract top players by arranging jobs for them at the university or in the city. On another level, even though I worked in the mail room, I very nearly lived the life of a professional rugby player – training most days and playing every Wednesday. This would be a way of life for me in years to come, and I had a foretaste of it in Sydney.

October soon came around. It was the end of the season and time for me to think about going back home to England – the country that I'd wanted to spend some time away from. I wanted to take myself out of the British/Irish way of life and be a part of the Australian way of life instead. Unfortunately, as much as I enjoyed the backpacking days of travelling around, they didn't submerge me in the Aussie way of life, because I hardly met any Australians! While travelling backpackers from other countries or from Britain were my social circle. It was good for me therefore to leave all that behind and settle into Sydney life. One guy, in particular, made me feel right at home in the city that was so far removed from my home in Kirby Grange. Andrew McInnerney played for Sydney University and we got on from the start. He took me home to his family and Sunday lunch with them was something special to look forward to! His friendship and his family's welcome gave me a longevity in Australia which I wouldn't have had as a backpacker. It was nice to be able to welcome him to my home when he came over to the UK. During my time in Sydney, I was able to turn away for a while from my English and Irish upbringing, and look at things in a way I hadn't done so before.

I was also away from mum and dad's guiding hands. I was away from the monks' steady, structured influence. I was out of my comfort zone, but that is where I wanted to be. But now was the right time to fly back and see where life would take me next.

8

Bricks, Contracts and some Nudity

IT WAS, WITHOUT doubt, the longest season of my rugby career. Starting in Sydney in April, then coming back to Harrogate in November and on until their season ended in May a year later. A thirteen-month season – that's got to be some sort of record!

As soon as I got back from down under it was back to work on the farm and rugby at Harrogate. I got into the first team not long after coming back and that was a good feeling. By the beginning of the 1996/97 season I was a first team regular. One memorable game that season was against Yorkshire rivals, Leeds, who were then a Third Division side. They had obvious plans to expand big time, and had invested heavily in creating a structure that would take them from the Third Division and beyond. They had lured former Wales and Scarlets forward, Phil Davies, to be their Director of Rugby and another Scarlet international, the fly-half Colin Stephens, had also travelled north with him. Phil won 46 caps for Wales and was an outstanding forward remembered, among other things, for playing a lead role in the battle of Cardiff. That was a particularly bad-tempered Wales v England encounter in 1987, which saw Phil take a punch from the massive England lock Wade Dooley.

We lost a crunching game against Phil Davies' Leeds. I had a bit of a ding-dong with Phil throughout the game and we were at each other for the eighty minutes, not always to the ref's satisfaction. We didn't talk to each other at all after the game as there was no obvious need to. I didn't know him personally, but I was aware of his Wales career. The talk in Yorkshire was that Leeds were trying to *buy* success at a time when everyone else was still playing the amateur game, training two nights a week after work. Whether that was a fair interpretation or not, Leeds were the only club in Yorkshire with any potential to go further. Leeds Tykes had been formed when Headingly and Roundhay rugby clubs were taken over, and ambition was plentiful there at that time.

For me, it was a case of finding my feet back home again, knuckling down on the farm and playing amateur rugby for Harrogate. I had no rugby career plan; the game didn't work like that in those days. One afternoon, I was sat on the forklift at home, as Guy and I were busy spreading fertiliser. My phone rang and a broad Welsh accent greeted me on the other end. It was Phil Davies. His words took me by surprise. He said that he'd been impressed with my game that day and wanted to meet me to discuss the possibility of offering me a professional playing contract with Leeds. I was amazed! I hadn't thought of earning a living from playing rugby at all. And it was a very exciting moment.

I told dad and he was over the moon. His reaction helped no end, but still, the doubts started to creep into my mind. Was this the right thing to do? Could it work? Would there be enough money for me to make a decent living? Was leaving the farm too much of a risk? Countless questions! Guy was already playing semi-professional rugby by then, having moved from Harrogate to Rotherham the year I returned from Australia. They were another Yorkshire team with ambition. Guy was working, but he was also being paid to play rugby. He was full of encouragement and knew a little bit more about what was involved.

The biggest consideration for both Guy and I was undoubtedly whether we were letting dad down. Were we stopping the continuation of the family business and shattering his hopes for the farm? Dad and mum had always been extremely supportive of us three children but this could now potentially be goodbye to all that. And Guy and I were considering such moves at about the same time. Would that make it harder for dad? He wasn't just losing two pairs of hands to work on the farm; we were his sons and that made all the difference. Until then, my perceived map of life had been playing rugby and helping to run the farm. My only aspiration as a rugby player was to play to the highest level of my ability. But playing rugby professionally was not an ambition for either of us.

Luckily, but not surprisingly, considering the background, dad's support was 100 per cent. But, not before he had given Phil Davies a thorough grilling about the set-up at Leeds! Phil called at the farm a few times, and dad gave him the third-degree about the structure of the club, its viability, his intentions for me, etc. Dad had reservations about Leeds because of the popularity of rugby league. The teams of both codes were to share the same ground and I think dad knew which one would be the weaker partner. He was also aware that Leeds United were a top football club with a huge following. Leeds Tykes, therefore, were creating something from nothing against tough opposition from two well-established teams. So he needed answers. I'm sure Phil thought that it was dad he was trying to sign in the end!

Phil was a visionary in terms of what he had planned for Leeds. He wouldn't just call at the house for chats, but phone both me and dad to explain his strategy. Phil realised that it was important to persuade my father as well as me. Even if I had made my mind up to go, he still wanted dad to be happy about it too. And I've always appreciated that.

So I signed my first professional contract in 1997. My time in Australia had played a big part in my decision, primarily because I'd been able to distance myself from the farm for a while. There was also the taster of the professional rugby set-up that I'd experienced at Sydney University. But apart from that, I knew that I could play rugby to a certain level, and believed enough in my own ability to want to push further. Guy and I also knew that we weren't leaving a job which we could never return to later, if needs be. The farm was always going to be there if we flopped completely as pro rugby players. Yet, we also had a deep sense of not wanting to let our parents down. They had given us every opportunity, and now this was a chance to take our rugby to a level higher than we'd imagined. They gave us their full support, and it would have been wrong to betray their faith in us.

In my case, I was aware that I hadn't maybe fulfilled academically what they had hoped for me. But, mum and dad never made us feel as though we owed them anything. However, I always had that niggling question in my mind, 'How could I repay their commitment to me?' Maybe Phil Davies had given me the chance to answer the question, so the professional contract was signed.

When I got to the Tykes, it was a professional set-up, in the sense that you were being paid, at least! The rest of the professional structure was, shall we say, a work in progress. To avoid the competition that dad and others feared, the Tykes decided to play their home games on a Sunday. Rugby league was played on Fridays, and football on Saturdays. And now there was a new sporting day-out for the people of Leeds. The squad was a mix of professionals and amateurs, with 15 of us signing pro terms and another 20 having jobs as well as playing for the team. This meant that the training sessions were always a mix, with those of us who were pros on our own during the day, and training with everyone else some evenings. As a result, there was a lot of down time for us.

Add this generous down time to the fact that the Headingly ground, where Leeds played, was in the student area of the city, and you get a clear picture of the life of a fresh-faced pro rugby player! But professionalism was a model that was being developed and professionalism, as an attitude, certainly hadn't kicked in yet. We were, to an extent, young rugby players with new-found money and status and not sure what to do with either. After every game on Sunday we would go out in the evening and then, after the Monday morning recovery session, we would meet at lunch times to go out on another drinking session. This would go through into Monday night. I became accustomed to local traditions very quickly and I soon learned about the Otley Run – a major pub crawl on the Otley Road out of Headingly towards Leeds. This run started at the top of the road and ended at the two pubs at the bottom, the Sky Rack and the Original Oak. This run was part of my weekly routine as a professional rugby player! One Monday afternoon, we were in the Original Oak, which was separated by a pedestrian crossing with traffic lights from the Sky Rack. That Monday I walked out of the Oak totally naked, not a stitch on me. I had folded all my clothes very neatly and was carrying them under my arm. A few of the others joined me. We stopped at the crossing at about 4.30 in the afternoon with all the rush hour traffic filling the road. We pressed the button and the light turned to red, as indeed did everyone else as we walked stark naked across one of Leeds' busiest roads in broad daylight! In to the Sky Rack pub we went and after placing my drinks order, I produced a £10 note for the barmaid from the top of the neatly folded clothes I was carrying.

On such nights I would stay at Colin Stephens' house instead of going home to the farm. But even such a good friend wasn't immune from my pranks after drinking. I got back after a session one night and couldn't wake Colin up to let me in. There was only one answer – I threw a brick through his living room window. When I got into the house, I realised that Colin was out all along, having stayed the night at his girlfriend's house. So I slept there and left in the morning before Colin returned, oblivious to the damage caused. When Colin did get back, all he saw was broken glass everywhere and a brick in his lounge! He had no idea it was me and thought he'd been the victim of some kind of vendetta or other.

That was all to the good in a fun kind of way, but word soon got back to the director of rugby at Leeds, my mate Phil Davies. He took me aside a few times and we had good heart-to-heart about the balance between responsibility and enjoyment and the importance of representing the club in public as well as on the field.

What did being a professional rugby player at Leeds mean? Nobody could tell us, so we made it up as we went along. In that first season, life and the rugby was pretty good!

9

A New Country

IF YOU'RE STARTING from scratch there's only one way you can build a team, and that's by buying players in – and buying big! That's what Phil Davies set about to do at Leeds. Today of course, there's a broader argument, and established teams sometimes choose that particular development path at the expense of encouraging new, young talent. For Phil however, there was no real alternative. Buying in to strengthen the squad would have to come first and the nurturing and development of new talent for the team would follow later. By the time Phil left, after ten years at the helm, the club had reached the Premiership. And then Academy players were an important part of the system as well.

It most certainly was a case of the United Nations at Leeds in those early days. Welshman Colin Stephens and ex-Ireland scrum-half, Christian Saverimutto, were early signings. Christian's father had been a leading player in the Sri Lankan rugby world, but his son was capped three times for Ireland. The New Zealand-born Tongan international full-back, Siteki Tuipulotu, also joined Leeds. He played in three World Cups for his country and is now a coach in Australia. But it was an Australian who grabbed the biggest attention – Wendell Sailor. He came to Leeds in my second season there, on a short-term contract at the end of his rugby league career. He joined for about 15 games – and was phenomenal! He was unstoppable and brought a lot to a developing club. He must have scored over 20 tries in his 15 matches and he certainly brought in the crowds, including some of the rugby league crowd as well. He was also there to give us the push towards promotion, which we actually didn't get that season – not that it was *his* entire fault!

Added to all this was the practice of signing all the best players from Yorkshire itself, and I resulted from that trawl. There were two guys at Harrogate who were starting to act as agents for players. They had seen the way that things were developing in the rugby world and ventured early into this new market while still playing and coaching. Ralph Zoing played for Harrogate with me and was an early pioneer in the world of rugby agencies, as was Adam Pearson – he went on to own Hull City Football Club and Derby County Football Club. These two were good friends and they sorted out my deal when I moved to Leeds. I was one of their first clients and they negotiated a contract of £15,000 a season for me. I was chuffed with that!

One of the first matches I remember playing in was a fourth round cup game against Leicester – my first taste of the really big time in a huge stadium in front of a packed house. We were stuffed by at least 50 points! This made me think that maybe Leeds wasn't going to take me far in terms of my rugby playing career. I was on the professional ladder, and my ambitions were now different because I was beginning to understand what it meant to be a professional rugby player. This thinking coincided with an upcoming contract renegotiation. The Leicester game made me look at my game in two ways. It made me ask myself whether I was actually good enough to carry on playing professionally (because we'd been so well beaten and I'd had a role to play in that). But also, it made me think what else was possible too. I could stay with Leeds of course and wait for them to be promoted to the top tier of rugby. But what if that took another couple of years? By then I would be nearing my late twenties. Guy was now playing for a Rotherham team who had reached two play-off finals. Maybe they would be the team that would make it to the highest level, not Leeds? So, one game generated many questions in my mind.

As I spent time thinking long and hard, I also felt huge admiration and gratitude to Phil Davies for taking a chance with me in the first place. He had plucked a 21 year-old from a Harrogate team and included me in his team-building at Leeds, giving me a chance to develop as a person as well.

The answer to my dilemma of whether to stay or go came about quite quickly in the end. I told Phil Davies that I was thinking of moving on. There were two options for me at that time: Rotherham was one and Leinster, potentially, another under the leadership of Mike Ruddock. But those clubs weren't actually professional at that point and the club/province structure had not been fully developed yet. In July 1998, Leinster came over for a pre-season English tour and I actually played for them against Nottingham. I went on their five-day training camp beforehand as well, and was very much part of their set-up.

However, Leeds offered me a three-year contract and the spiel that came with it was very flattering indeed! I was told that they would like to build the team around me, a local Yorkshire lad, and I could take the team forward. But just as I knew that I had to leave Yorkshire for a while and go to Australia I also knew that I had to leave Leeds. It was time for pastures new.

But as deliberate as this thinking was, the actual move itself came about by accident. My agent at the time, Alastair Saverimutto, happened to hear that Llanelli were looking for a back-row player. When he told me about Llanelli, the thought of joining a Welsh club wasn't even on the radar for me. But, certainly, here was a possible opportunity. It was Phil Davies' former club; Colin Stephens' and Paul Jones' too. So I knew enough about it. But ironically, they had little to do with my link to the Scarlets at all.

One Friday afternoon I headed down to the far reaches of west Wales, to the world-famous Stradey Park rugby ground to have talks with the coach, the renowned Gareth Jenkins. This visit was with dad's blessing, as his earlier reservations about Leeds were still in the back of my mind. However, he saw the Scarlets as a viable option for me. I'd heard that Dafydd James was on his way there, and that Scott Quinnell was coming back to play for the club having left Richmond. Ironically, this also created a new opportunity for me: Richmond needed a new Number 8 and joining them would have been an option for me at that time too, and they did offer me a contract. That would have been good, as Guy was playing for London Scottish by then. But, I decided to plough my own furrow.

Llanelli's ambition was obvious. I was totally sold

on Stradey as a rugby ground. I vaguely knew of the history of the club, but wasn't aware of their famous victory against the All Blacks in 1972. Saying that now almost feels like a confession of wrong-doing, such is the honoured place that that victory has in the folklore of Welsh rugby. However, I soon got to know about it! I *was* aware of them conquering the Aussies in the 1992/93 season, winning the league and being voted the best club team in Britain. Phil Davies made sure I knew about that because he was there!

But, as far as their current set-up was concerned, I was only conscious of what I'd seen on *Rugby Special* with Nigel Starmer-Smith commentating! That was enough though to give me a good indication of the style of rugby played at Stradey. I didn't know a great deal about the surrounding area either. When I visited I realised that it wasn't a big city and that was a huge bonus for me. Along with Gareth Jenkins, I also met team manager, Anthony Buchanan, and chief executive Stuart Gallagher. All three were convincing. To be honest, no hard sell was actually needed. I could see that it would be a shop window for me as far as the international scene was concerned. And there was the bait of European rugby if I got into the first team as well. All this of course meant that I would have to take myself out of my comfort zone. It was another massive challenge.

I went home on Friday evening with all these thoughts mulling around in my head. By Monday, a written contract had been drawn up. I travelled down to meet Anthony Buchanan at a Midlands hotel. And that was it! I was now a Llanelli player and, at about exactly the same time, Guy moved to Welsh club Ebbw Vale after London Scottish folded.

In the space of a couple of weeks I'd gone from being offered a new contract at Leeds to signing for a club in a part of the world I knew little about. I suppose if anything had come of Leinster's pre-season tour of England, I might well have gone to play for them and not headed to west Wales. But they didn't show any interest and that, by now, is one of life's 'what ifs?' Phil Davies wasn't exactly happy when I said that I wanted to leave Leeds. But when I later told him where I was going, I think it was a case of, well if you're going anywhere, it might as well be Llanelli. I don't think he would have been too pleased if I'd gone to Rotherham – that would have been a bit like a Man Utd player transferring to Liverpool! I think he was secretly happy that the Scarlets would be my new club.

He was obviously able to tell me so much about the Scarlets and he gave me a lot of useful advice and insightful comments. He also knew of my ambition to play for Ireland and it was obvious that that dream was more likely to come true playing for a region which competed regularly against Irish clubs in the Celtic League.

So this kid with an English accent, who wanted to play for Ireland, landed in Wales.

10

A Scarlet Life
and Some Traditions

I WAS, THEREFORE, a Scarlet. Each day spent as part of the set-up showed me a little more about what that actually meant: how each Llanelli squad fitted into that impressive lineage which had started way back in 1872. It couldn't have been in starker contrast to Leeds Tykes, who were beginning from scratch and bringing players in from all over the place to establish a new team. Llanelli was heritage on a rugby pitch.

I remember exactly when that sense of a legacy began to kick-in for me. It was the 2000 Welsh Cup final against Swansea in the brand new Millennium Stadium, Cardiff. Llanelli had an amazing record in Welsh Cup competitions, be it the original WRU Challenge Cup, the Schweppes Cup or the SWALEC Cup. By the time of the 2000 final, it was called the WRU Challenge Cup and Llanelli had won it ten times since 1972. In 1999, the Wales international centre, Scott Gibbs, had stirred things up between the two finalists, saying that when the two teams had met in that year's final, and Swansea had won 37–10, it had been a case of 'men against boys'! He still stood by his words when challenged to withdraw them. So, it was 'game on' in 2000! We carried that niggle into the final. The word revenge is often used, and we needed no more motivation than Scott's words! And that, despite having the greatest rugby motivator, Gareth Jenkins, as our coach. We won the 2000 final 22–12 and the cup was ours once more.

I knew then that I had arrived at a club with something more to it than the norm. The league set-up was fairly new then, and the cup final day was evidently a much revered tradition for the Scarlets and their amazingly loyal fans. I played in the semi-final of the cup that year at the Millennium Stadium as well, but the final day itself was something else. It was a late kick-off, a club game, yet there were around 60,000 supporters there, and I found that to be incredible. I thought to myself, I've arrived! Another competition, the European Cup, had not long been established, and we were doing well in that tournament too. I felt the same emotion and pride in a night game in January, with the new millennium just two weeks old, in a packed Stradey Park, when we defeated Wasps 25–15. The visit to the Madjeski Stadium to play Northampton in the European competition was also a wonderful day. And seeing how many fans had travelled up the M4 to see that match was amazing.

European rugby was starting to catch the imagination of the fans. The WRU Cup, however, was completely different. Playing in a final for Llanelli made me realise how big the club were in the cup tradition. I saw what rugby meant to the town and the area. This amazing local passion for the game became even more evident when we travelled back to Llanelli after the match. I didn't know it at the time, but there was a certain tradition associated with the Scarlets' cup wins. As soon as the celebrations on the pitch were over, we lifted the cup aloft and did our laps of honour. The cup was then put back in its case and placed on the bus for the journey back west. On the trip home, the cup was taken out of its case at exactly the same spot: the bridge over the river Loughor on the M4, a river which marks the divide between west Wales and the rest of south Wales. At that very point, the cup was lifted as high as you can (in a coach!) by wild and excited players, cheering and shouting with gusto! And only then were we allowed to really celebrate. That was amazing – a special ritual. And now, *I* was a part of it too! Gareth Jenkins would then top the whole thing off with a rendition of 'Far away the hills are calling', his special cup song. Then the partying really started! It must have been a long wait for the players when they won the cup in 1998 at Bristol's Ashton Gate. But even then, the tradition was honoured. Crossing the Severn Bridge back into Wales wasn't the appropriate place to start the celebrations; they had to wait to cross the Loughor! That was what clinched the heritage.

As time went by, I became very aware of the successes that the club had achieved. I knew that they'd beaten the All Blacks in 1972 and Australia in 1993, but these impressive statistics were never forced down our throats as players (apart maybe from Rupert 'Moonie' Moon reliving his 1993 glory days for us, time and time again!). But references to past exploits were not over-bearing, as we had to focus on the present day. As I said, European rugby was developing and the league in Wales was changing as well. It was a new millennium and it felt like a new era. We would never want to forget the past, but we also felt that we needed to add to what had gone before.

My first week in Wales wasn't spent in Llanelli at all. I travelled down from Leeds with my now former Leeds team-mate, Colin Stephens, who was visiting Llanelli for the weekend. My accommodation arrangements hadn't been finalised in time, so I ended up staying with new team-mate Rhodri Davies and his family in the small market town of Llandeilo, in the north of Carmarthenshire. This was a great time, and it was a bit of a buffer being able to stay with a family and not having to share a house with strangers straightaway. However, accommodation plans soon kicked in after that, and I ended up living with Matt Cardey, another new player, who was a Kiwi and had joined from the Newport club.

We lived in a house in the Coedcae area of Llanelli. He'd arrived before me, so I walked in and was greeted by a guy with long, curly, ginger locks and a broad New Zealand accent. OK, I thought to myself, what's going on here! It was indeed strange that we were thrown together, the Kiwi and the Yorkshireman, but thankfully, we both got on really well. We were nearly the same age – our birthdays are two weeks apart. We were both new to the club at the same time, so we could help each other settle in. We shared everything that was new and supported each other throughout. And that made it easier for us both to concentrate on the main task – keeping a regular place in the first team. And, Matt was one of the best men at my wedding too.

We both joined Scarlets at the beginning of the 1999 World Cup campaign. Many established first team players weren't at the club when we arrived, as they were on World Cup duty. Stephen Jones wasn't there and Neil Boobyer, Chris Wyatt and Scott Quinnell were also missing from the squad. So, we were thrown in the deep end at training sessions with really experienced players who weren't part of the Wales set-up then: players such as Ian Boobyer, John Davies and Wayne Proctor. The training sessions at Scarlets were not all that different from Leeds, to be honest. Peter Herbert was the conditioning coach at the Scarlets at the time, and I think Phil Davies had taken a lot of what Peter did at the club with him to Leeds. There was a synergy between the two set-ups.

My first game in a Scarlet shirt was against a Hungarian XV overseas. This tour, in my mind, proved invaluable to the successes we experienced during the following years. This was a great experience for us guys who were not only new to the club but also new to this level of rugby. It meant that we could integrate into an environment that wasn't all just about training – and then going home at night. We had to spend time trying to get to know each other, which meant relaxing and having a few beers as well as taking part in the hard training sessions and matches.

The mastermind behind this approach to build a cohesive team was our legendary coach, Gareth Jenkins. We trained hard and we played hard. Having thirty-five, forty people together for eight days was quite intense and not the usual set-up that any of us were used to, and we were in a foreign country too. We spent a couple of days in Budapest and then visited the countryside. This whole way of working was less common then than it is nowadays. It was pre-season training but with a tour feel to it as well. This tour convinced me that Gareth

Jenkins' reputation as being one of the best motivators in the game was wholly deserved. He had the knack of saying the right things at the right time to the right player. To do that year in year out with a squad of so many different players is simply quite a remarkable gift to have. He was always able to keep things fresh, game after game. He also had an unbelievable knowledge of all matters to do with rugby. We were, in fact, trained in a completely different way to what I'd experienced at Leeds. Gareth was much more of an instinctive coach on training days; he watched what was going on in front of him and reacted to that. In a sense he was less planned and organised. But it would be completely wrong to say that he didn't know what was going on as the training sessions developed. He knew what he wanted us to achieve – yet, he would let us find out for ourselves what that was! However, I suppose that did run the risk of not being effective but, more often than not, it did work extremely well. He gave us the freedom to play our own game within a team situation – which can be a risky way, but his record speaks for itself. So, I went from Leeds' structured, textbook training method to Gareth's way! 'Find your own way under my guidance' was the Gareth's way of thinking. And, he was always in control.

In that first season, his triumph at putting together a mixture of rookies and experienced players as a team was evident. We made the semi-finals of the European Cup, we won that Welsh Cup again by beating arch rivals Swansea, and we did reasonably well in the league too. His way certainly worked. No doubt Gareth's attitude was nurtured from another rugby great – the legend that was Carwyn James. Carwyn was the only coach to lead the Lions to a series win overseas, in New Zealand; he also coached the Llanelli Scarlets to their famous win against the All Blacks in 1972 – a game in which Gareth played. Carwyn's famous quote was that rugby was 'a thinking man's game' and Gareth put his own spin on that approach. Gareth's longevity in rugby coaching is almost unheard of within the game today, and it's sad that his time as Wales' coach didn't match up to the expectation. And personally, I don't think that was *all* Gareth's responsibility.

His methods also transferred to the international stage. On the Lions tour to New Zealand, I know that two of my fellow Irish internationals, Paul O'Connell and Donncha O'Callaghan, said that Gareth's speech before the first game reduced them to tears because it was so passionate. That's not bad for a guy who hadn't been a Lion himself, yet could still instil that sense of pride into those who had been chosen that year. He had a unique way of coaching and his motivational skills were second to none.

But, with the serious training, there was never a shortage of fun when Gareth was around either. There were always little incidents, week in, week out, that would make us smile or laugh outright, and no shortage of players who would be the first to crack-up because of something Gareth did or said.

We continued with trips to Hungary and Slovenia for the next few years and they proved to be very successful. I remember one trip for reasons other than the rugby! Guy – also in the club at the time – and I had organised a court session for the whole squad, which issued hefty fines for offences we decided that members had committed! For example, we made Gareth Jenkins and Dai Chips, the physio, dress up in a tight, leopard-skin miniskirt (having done quite well to find one that actually fitted, to be honest)! But, things got a little out of hand. After the court session in a downstairs room of the hotel, we went upstairs where there was a piano in the hotel bar. Residents and locals were relaxing in there, but suddenly they were confronted by a full squad of rugby players. One of the lads, known on such social occasions by his alter ego name of Dilwyn, was a little worse for wear and started to urinate near the piano in front of everyone. Gareth, at that very moment on his way to stop Guy from doing something silly, saw this out of the corner of his eye. He changed tack and went over to stop Dilwyn. But, as he did so, he slipped on the liquid which had been deposited on the floor and took Dilwyn out with him as he fell over. So there was Dilwyn and a leopard-skin miniskirted Gareth Jenkins wrestling in urine on the floor of a Hungarian hotel! It was absolutely hysterical! The next day, however, Gareth called us together and talked to us about our behaviour and responsibility, how we need to act as level-headed team members. But he'd been game enough to go along with his punishment of wearing the miniskirt, yet he knew quite well where the line was, and when it had been crossed.

However, with his miniskirt packed away, we went on to enjoy a run of a few good seasons under his unique leadership. That first season was amazing for me. I never thought that I'd get the chance to play with legends such as Scott Quinnell, Stephen Jones and Garan Evans, players whom I'd watched before arriving at Stradey. Now I was in the same team as them.

It was still very much a transitional time as far as

rugby was concerned. Not quite amateur but not fully professional either. For example, the team's hooker at Stradey, now Wales forwards coach Robin McBryde, still had a day job with an electricity company. So it was a mix – there were those of us who were professionals training between 1 p.m. and 3 p.m. in the afternoon and then others who would join us in the evening after work. Therefore, there was plenty of down time, which meant late nights and lie-ins.

I didn't really get to know the area around Llanelli that well during my free time in those early days, nor the nation that was Wales, and its culture. I was, however, aware that I was in a land where another language was spoken. The fourth television channel, S4C, had already been broadcasting in Wales for about seventeen years before I moved to Wales. My arrival in Wales also coincided with a huge resurgence in all things Welsh, from music and the arts to the language itself, as well as political devolution. At Llanelli, quite a few players and staff spoke Welsh from day-to-day: there was the inimitable and infectious Grav, Stephen Jones, Robin McBryde and a few others. Those of us who weren't able to speak the language didn't have an issue with those who did, even if they spoke it in front of us. They weren't speaking Welsh in order to exclude us, be rude, or be ignorant – they were just speaking their first language. I liked that. I liked the fact that we were considered the Welsh-speaking club. It gave us an extra 'something' and it made other teams feel a little less welcome when they came to play against us! It added, and still adds to our mystique as a rugby team. This was an important aspect of the club and this feeling for the Welsh language became more and more important the longer I stayed at Llanelli. But, I didn't think for one second, however, that in years to come I would have a wife and two children whose mother tongue was Welsh.

11

Clubs, Caps and Achilles' Heels

AFTER SUCH A successful and enjoyable first season, I returned from the summer break raring to go and pick up where I'd left off. Imagine the heartache, therefore, when it soon became apparent that my second season would be curtailed by injury and it would keep me off the pitch for a long time.

I played one pre-season game at the beginning of August, which went OK. But, at a training session soon afterwards, everything changed. We were doing an old-style conditioning test called the 'bleep test' at a gym in Llanelli's town centre. I was doing fine, reaching level 15 comfortably, which is at the high end. I do recall turning over on the same ankle several times, but thought nothing more of it. The next thing I heard (and all the other lads in the gym with me), was a loud noise as though someone had fired a gun in the gym. I knew instantly that something was wrong. I'd fallen over, had tried to get up but had tumbled again. We all knew what had happened – such a sound is an obvious indicator that the Achilles tendon has gone – and completely gone. A simple test on the floor of the gym confirmed the worst. I was asked to move my foot, and if there was a connection between the foot and the Achilles, my lower leg muscles would show that – there was none.

So, I was off to Morriston Hospital in Swansea where the team surgeon, Bob Leyshon, confirmed the worst. That same evening, I went under the knife so that my Achilles could be repaired. One minute I going to the gym with the lads as normal, but a few hours later, an operation on an injury would put a stop to my rugby career for a long time. With that change, a whole host of other thoughts and feelings came flooding to mind. It dawned on me that I could be facing a whole season out of the game. I began to realise what exactly that would mean for me in terms of my rugby aspirations, and how that fact could play on my mind. The psychology of a long-term injury is as much a part of recuperation and rehabilitation as the physical aspect, if not more. Everything had been blown out of the water by a fateful turn of the ankle. How I would deal with this could change the course of my playing career. The day I left hospital was the beginning of a long haul to get back to normality.

Until that point, I hadn't had a serious injury. A hand operation while at Leeds was about it – apart from, of course, cutting my finger open on a farm tractor when I was three! But this was very different. At the time of the injury, the Achilles was dealt with quite differently from the way it's dealt with nowadays. Today, you can expect to be laid up for about four or five months with such an injury, but then, you were looking at being out of action for a whole season. An immediate worry for me, therefore, was my contract. I had signed for two years. I had already played for one year but was now in the situation of not being able to fulfil the second half my contracted period – and that was a huge worry. Would they renew my contract having only seen me play for a year? Potentially, I could be out of a job as soon as I had recovered from the injury. What other team would take the risk of signing me knowing that I had just recovered from a serious injury and had not played for a year? It was early days in terms of professional rugby, and I didn't have such a thing as medical cover or injury insurance and that was a worry too. The mind games were kicking in, big time.

I had to constantly remind myself that I'd had a great deal of game time in that first season which hopefully would stand me in good stead. People had seen enough of me, I hoped, to know what I could do. That's the hope that I clung on to in that dreadful time.

But there was another dark cloud hanging over me as well. At the end of my first season with the Scarlets, Ireland came knocking on my door again and asked me to go with the Irish squad on their American tour to Canada, the USA and Argentina. I had already featured in their previous Six Nations campaign, but more of that later. I played in all three Tests on that tour, beating the USA, drawing with Canada, but losing to Argentina. In the second match of the tour, against the USA, a huge bonus was that my brother made his debut and he and I both scored two tries. That was an amazing feeling. The phone conversation with Clive Woodward was most certainly a distant memory by then.

By the end of that season, I felt as though I was making an impact and beginning to secure my place in

Warren Gatland's Irish team. But now, all that too was in jeopardy, as I was laid up with an injury. Would Ireland still want me? Would I be able to restart my international career again? These questions weighed heavily on my mind.

There was also another tantalising thought plaguing my sub-conscious too. There would be a Lions tour in 2001. I'd been part of the Ireland set-up in the summer of 2000 and therefore in a position to draw the attention of the Lions' selectors also. I have no idea if I would have made it, had I been fit. Graham Henry was the Lions' coach, and he would have seen me play a great deal because of his involvement with Wales' national side and the Welsh clubs. A good second season at the Scarlets could have consolidated my position. Not having the chance to prove myself to potential selectors, however, was so frustrating. And of course, when the team selection was made, it was agonising to sit and wonder what might have been. Frustration isn't the word!

Imagine my feelings therefore, when word got back to me that Graham Henry had told a mutual acquaintance that I would have been seriously considered, had I not been injured. I went through a few more 'bleep tests' of my own at that point, and they had nothing to do with timings!

If there was a silver lining to all this – and it's a very dubious one, at that – then it was the fact that my team-mate and housemate, Matt Cardey, suffered serious ligament damage and dislocated his ankle in the same pre-season. Once again, that meant that we could support each other, two crocks in the same house! It also meant that I didn't have to depend 100 per cent on him to do everything around the house. We could hobble around tending to each other on an equal footing, pardon the pun!

We both, fairly early on, thought that it would be a good idea for us to get out of the club environment and look for an element of rehabilitation elsewhere. We suggested the Sports Injury Rehab at the Lilleshall National Sports Centre in Shropshire. It's the longest established and the biggest sports injury rehab centre in Britain. In the past it's looked after the England football team and other top athletes. Matt and I thought that moving away from the day-to-day situation in Llanelli for a short while would help us deal with our injuries better. It would make us less inward looking and lift us out of the gloom which comes with serious injuries. The club agreed, and I was scheduled to go there first.

I had, up until that point, spent eight weeks in plaster. I came out of the plaster on the Friday and was to go to Lilleshall the following Monday. So, to celebrate being out of plaster and going to a top-quality rehab centre, I had a night out in Cardiff on the Saturday. I was on crutches of course and, as I walked up some stairs at a nightclub in Cardiff, I slipped and twisted the injured ankle again. I wasn't sure what the extent of the damage was, so off I went to Lilleshall on the Monday morning, as planned. After a few days there, they decided that I had significantly harmed the Achilles again, and told me that there was no point in my being there any longer.

That was a really low point for me. I had dealt well with the injury for eight weeks. Then, I had gone out for a few beers with friends and made things worse. I was pretty sick with myself, more than anything, and gave myself a hard time for letting it happen. It was all made worse when I realised that I'd have to go back under the knife again. The Achilles was so damaged that I needed another operation. The original incident had caused my Achilles to be 95 per cent damaged. This second incident had caused it to be about 30 per cent damaged. Not as bad, but bad enough.

Looking back, it was probably stupid of me to go on that night out, but I thought I would be fine on crutches, and I certainly needed something to relieve the boredom of the previous weeks laid up with my injury. This setback meant that I would be in plaster for another five or six weeks. I was gutted.

Matt was out of his cast by the time I was out of plaster for the second time. So, we both asked to go to Lilleshall again. The club agreed and we went there for a week. It was intensive rehab, to say the least. We had physio morning, afternoon and evening. There were games and exercises to do throughout the day. It was an amazing facility and we both benefited immensely, and went there a few more times after that initial visit. The club probably weren't completely at ease about sending us there. It did mean extra costs of course, as well as other considerations. But I am still really grateful that they did agree to the Lilleshall stay. It was exactly what was needed.

My brother had joined the Scarlets by this time as well, which was great for me. I couldn't wait to get out on the pitch and play alongside him. He had also moved in with Matt and me. So, for the first time in years we lived together again. But, not long after he signed, he broke his leg! So there we were: three crocks on crutches in the same house, which we instantly renamed the Cursed

House!

Now, there were three of us dealing with long-term lower limb injuries. We certainly had a laugh about that and had a good time at the house. There was a swimming pool in the back garden which helped, and we had plenty of personal space. And we got on great together. We had a very effective way of making sure that we ate proper meals. We would invite friends round, quite often Welsh internationals and British Lions, such as Stephen Jones and Dwayne Peel, and made sure that they ended up doing the cooking! Simple but effective! Strange then, that they both have since gone on to open a restaurant with my good friend Robert Williams. Maybe their love of food came from our injuries! We weren't too bad as cooks either, especially Matt, who was a genius with Sunday roast dinners. Guy and I tended to stick to the pastas and stir-fries. But when the injuries kicked in, it could have been so easy to fall back on microwave meals as easier options.

As it became clearer that the injury was now getting better, I sought some advice from Tim Atter, a specialist physio in Cardiff. During our first meeting, he didn't ask me anything about my Achilles. He just wanted to know when I thought I could play again. Could I play that season? Was I up for it? Did I want it enough? That was a mentally tough process to go through. I thought that maybe I should leave my return to competitive rugby until the start of the next season (September 2001), so that my leg would be completely healed by then. But Tim thought it was worth trying to get me ready for the last few games of the 2000/01 season, in order to get my confidence back. When I first met Tim, I was still stumbling around the house for five or six minutes after getting out of bed every morning. Tim gave me the confidence to aim for those last few games of the season, and the confidence to push and work really hard towards it, even though there were times when I wasn't sure if what I was doing was good for my leg at all.

As it turned out, I was back on the pitch at the end of April 2001 and I played two games. I'd sustained my injury at the beginning of August 2000. I was so glad that I'd made the April return as it obviously gave me match time, but also the appetite to work on my fitness and skills before the next season. Fortunately, the club had agreed to renew my contract as well, so that worry had been taken away from me. The pieces were beginning to fall into place once again.

Having been through nine months of physical injury and mental anguish, there was one experience which helped put all that had happened in perspective. During the summer of 2001, after playing those two games, I went to Spala in Poland with Warren Gatland and the Ireland team. (Incidentally, that's where he took the Welsh boys this year before the 2011 World Cup, in order to work on fitness and conditioning.) Spala a very spartan place, a long way from anywhere, and the training we had there was intense. But the event during the trip which left its mental mark on me was an excursion to Auschwitz, one afternoon. This was also something that the Welsh boys did when they went to Spala.

I found the whole experience of visiting Auschwitz mentally anguishing. The whole place was eerie, devoid of any spirit or life. No birds sang. People who'd already been there had warned me that's how it would be, but I had no comprehension of what they meant until I actually visited myself. I saw the cells where mothers and children were held, the hundreds and hundreds of suitcases with their tags still in place showing the names of various towns and villages throughout Europe, the hundreds of pairs of glasses, the human hair and the children's shoes. I think we all found it extraordinarily moving. On that trip we might well have complained about how tough things were for us, but the ice chambers we endured in training were nothing compared to the gas chambers suffered by over a million people at Auschwitz. It was only a short visit, but it was mentally intensive and left a long-lasting impression. I'm glad I did it, because it made me realise that what I'd seen was a part of the world that I now lived *happily* in, and it put my complaints about injuries into total perspective.

12

Tigers and Benefactors

ONE TEAM DOMINATED my first full season back as a fully-fit player, and they were the Leicester Tigers. We were drawn in the same group of the Heineken European Cup. The first group stage game was away at Leicester and we were well up for it that day. The Scarlets brand of rugby is known for being open and flowing, and this particular season we had a pack of forwards who were big and could compete against any team renowned for their pack power. During the first line-out against Leicester that day, I remember our huge American second row, Luke Gross, throwing Martin Johnson aside like a rag doll. That set the benchmark for the rest of the game. At that point, Leicester were the reigning European champions having beaten Stade Français 34–30 in the final in France. We were under no illusions, therefore, on our trip to Leicester, but neither were we intimidated. We gave them a tough game and were unlucky to come away with a narrow defeat, 12–9. At the back of my mind was the memory that I had played for Leeds at this ground, and been totally stuffed. That match had been my first taste of a big occasion, but this one was bigger, and the performance and the score were a little bit more respectable.

In the second week of January 2002, it was Leicester's turn to come down to Stradey Park. In the interim, we'd had a good run, winning six of our nine games since our visit to the Midlands.

We didn't, however, get the best preparation for meeting the European champions this time. A week before their visit, we were well beaten by Perpignan, 42–10. The rugby press wrote us off, giving us no hope against the Tigers after such a defeat. But, we took the game to them up-front, to such an extent that players like Neil Back were constantly moaning to the referee about our aggressive approach. Martin Johnson commented after the match that it had been one of his toughest. We obviously got under their skin and won comfortably in the end, 24–12. The *Telegraph* summed the whole occasion up quite nicely the following day:

> It was a special day at Stradey Park yesterday, almost a throwback to the days before leagues when a match between the top English and Welsh sides was enough by itself to galvanise rugby-mad communities.
>
> The Llanelli folk even managed to push a piano on to the pitch before kick-off in order to spice up the sing-song, and it made a welcome change from the pyrotechnics and scantily-clad dancing girls which usually accompany big games these days.

The rugby was highly complimented as well, as was our attitude to the game, with my brother Guy getting a special mention from former England lock and now rugby correspondent, Paul Ackford:

The game turned Llanelli's way and they were so confident 15 minutes into the second half that Guy Easterby forsook a very kickable penalty when the score was 18–12 in Llanelli's favour to take a quick tap penalty. It appeared an act of madness at the time. No one is that generous to the European champions, but Easterby obviously knew something which the rest of us did not.

The victory meant that we were through to the quarter-finals and we were drawn to meet Bath. The game on the Saturday was called off because of torrential rain and a waterlogged pitch. So we had to stay overnight and play the game on the Sunday. I woke up in our hotel on that Sunday with mixed feelings. It was good to see that the rain had stopped and that the game was on. But having hung around the hotel all day on Saturday, not knowing if the game was on or not for hours on end, we wondered if that would play on our minds. Had we missed our opportunity and had the moment gone? Thankfully, that was not the case, and we won, 27–10. And our reward for reaching the semi-final of the European Cup – another game against Leicester!

Llanelli were attracting a lot more attention now. People were taking notice of what we were achieving on the pitch and nothing does that more, as far as the London press is concerned anyway, than two back-to-back victories over English clubs. The semi-final was to be played on a neutral ground, the City Ground, Nottingham, home of Nottingham Forest football team. This was the first ever rugby game played there, and it meant a lot to me. I had supported Nottingham Forest throughout my teens, oddly, because my brother had decided that I should! He supported Liverpool and I wanted to as well, but he wasn't too happy about little brother following the same team as him – so he decided I should support Forest! Despite this being forced upon me, it was a golden age for Forest football under the unique Brian Clough, and I ended up following his team with fervour in the end. So, it was a huge honour to go to that ground with the Scarlets, and play on the pitch where some of my footballing heroes had played and won a league title, two European Cups and four League Cups under the genius that was Brian Clough.

The sheer number of Scarlets fans who'd made the journey to Nottingham had a huge impact on me and the rest of the team. It was a neutral ground, and although Nottingham isn't that far from Leicester, I'm sure that our fans filled half the stadium that day. It gave us such a boost as players – it was unbelievable.

On top of all that, of course, there was a certain history between us and Leicester to 'up the ante' significantly that day. It was one win apiece going into that day, and the victor this time would be in the European Cup final. We carried on where we'd left off at Stradey, and had them on the rack early on. But then, for some reason, our level of play dipped a little. However, we managed to keep our noses in front and, with the full eighty minutes on the clock, we were leading 12–10. In injury time, there was a scrum inside their half, and we were penalised for an infringement. Tim Stimpson stepped up to take a long-range penalty. He gave it all he had and it hit the upright, bounced onto the crossbar and dropped over on the right side for the three points. The whistle blew, the game was over, and 13–12 to them. What a cruel way to settle a match! We were devastated. Not getting over the Leicester line that day was a huge mental blow for us as a club. We had been building a reputation in Europe; we were going somewhere and making others take notice. With the group of players that we had then, it was our opportunity to go all the way. To fall that close to the final, in such a manner, was hard to take. Again, the *Telegraph* summed it up a day later:

> How those gods enjoy making merry sport of Llanelli. If sadism is your thing, then Nottingham was the place to be. The misery of others makes for great drama, painful as it was for the spirited Scarlets. The Marquis de Sade must be a Tigers fan.

One of the features of the developing game in those days was having to play at the highest level on more than one front. With the Leicester game behind us, we still had a Welsh Cup final to look forward to and a chance to win the Welsh League. So, there was no time to lick our wounds, no time to relax. It was a case of having to maintain the intensity, despite the adversity. We managed to do so against Cardiff in the last league game of the season, when we needed a win to secure the league. With fifteen minutes left on the clock, we were 25–6 behind and well out of it, it seemed. But we found some reserves from somewhere and scored twenty points in that last period to win 26–25. The league championship was ours, at least.

The Welsh Cup final, however, was one game too many for us. After all the effort against Leicester, the comeback against Cardiff, there wasn't enough fuel left in the tank to beat Pontypridd in the final. We lost 17–20. That was disappointing for us because of the status the Welsh Cup had in the club's heritage. The cup meant a lot to us and to the fans that were used to a good day out in Cardiff on cup final day. We felt we'd let them down. We did bounce back the following season, though and won yet another cup for Llanelli, the twelfth by then, and the fans had their winning day out again!

The Leicester, Cardiff and Ponty games were all played within less than three weeks. It was a big ask to expect three top performances from our side. After such big matches, the professional players were all back in training and focusing on the next game the following day. Those who were still semi-professionals were back to work on Monday morning. The structure was imbalanced. Changes were afoot and the end of the 2002/03 season saw club rugby, as we'd known it in Wales, come to an end. A century and more of tradition had concluded.

Personally, I'd enjoyed a brilliant time at Llanelli before regionalisation came in. We'd been involved in two European Cup semi-finals, won the league once and the Welsh Cup twice. If anyone had told me, when I left Leeds, that this is how it would turn out, I'm not sure if I would have believed them. It is a shame that we couldn't secure the Heineken European Cup that year. Winning the Heineken, the league and the Welsh Cup would have made us a great team and, in terms of Llanelli, would have put us right up there with the team of the 1992/93 season who were, at the time, the best in Britain. That didn't happen, but we did enjoy great success and I was really glad to be part of it.

When restructuring was announced, the talk was that we would be amalgamated with arch rivals Swansea. That would have been difficult because of the history of the two clubs but, more than that, from a players' perspective, there were too many good players at both clubs to merge them into one. It made sense, therefore, that Llanelli should stand alone. Geographically, we had a huge region to the west and north of us to look after, and that area would have been neglected had we been joined to the team representing the city to the east of us. We were fortunate that club Chief Executive Stuart Gallagher and club Chairman Huw Evans fought a hard battle to keep our identity. Certainly, as players, we never had the attitude that we were better than everyone else, and needed to be apart as a result. Our attitude was, quite simply, that we had been building a strong team together for a few seasons by then; we were creating something which had given us a strong enough identity to stand alone. That's how *we* saw it.

Regionalisation had to happen because there wasn't the quality of players, nor the strength in depth to sustain more than four or five teams. Many have commentated since that this set-up doesn't promote strong competition for places in the Welsh squad if there are only four or five players competing for any place. But, when there were twelve clubs in the old system, that competition was diluted anyway because of the standard of the teams competing against each other. I don't think that the standard of the player base has gone down since regional rugby came about.

There is room to question, however, how successful the regional system has been in Wales when you look at the changes in other countries and the successes they've enjoyed, specifically in the Heineken European Cup. Irish regions have won that top European competition four times since regionalisation: Munster have won it twice, as have Leinster. The best performance by any

Welsh club has been Cardiff reaching the finals against Toulouse in 1996, prior to English and Scottish clubs joining the competition.

It does beg the question, then, why have the Irish regions been so successful? I think that Wales have missed a trick actually, by not contracting their players centrally as happens in Ireland. Irish players are contracted to the Irish Rugby Football Union (IRFU) on either an international or provincial contract. There are payment bands within these structures too, so that players such as Brian O'Driscoll and Ronan O'Gara would be on one amount and other, less experienced players, in a different remuneration package.

This whole system allows the IRFU to protect its players from speculative approaches from clubs outside Ireland and it certainly benefits the provinces. For example, if an international player has had what the IRFU management deem to be too much game time, they can step in and ask him not to play. This protects the player obviously, but it also helps the province in the long run as well. That's not to say that there hasn't been any friction between provincial coaches and the IRFU management. But, by now, it seems to be a successful system that works. One obvious example is the fact that the IRFU has been extremely successful in holding on to its big stars: Brian O'Driscoll, Ronan O'Gara, Paul O'Connell and a host of others would be targets for the rich French clubs. In previous years they would have been the target of top English clubs as well. When I was playing rugby in my early twenties, there was no shortage of Irish international players at English clubs. But, by now, none of the experienced, world-class Irish stars play their club rugby outside Ireland.

That's because they are contracted to an IRFU which is financially stronger. On their own, the provinces would not be able to fund the wages of these players. Now they can be paid handsomely enough to not want to leave their homeland.

There is another factor to consider also, in that the Irish Government, the Dail, passed a law some years ago giving tax incentives to sportsmen. For years artists and musicians had enjoyed tax breaks and now it's been extended to the world of sport. There is a belief that such people work really hard; they can earn a great deal of money for a short time, but there are no guarantees of earnings later on. They now know that at the end of their career, they will get 15 per cent of their earnings back from the best ten years of their careers. It's that sort of incentive which has helped stars such as U2 and Enya remain in Ireland, and it's worked well for rugby players too.

In the last five or six years, only a handful of players have left an Irish province to play for a foreign club. Leo Cullen and Shane Jennings went to Leicester, but they weren't getting a lot of game time with their province at that stage. Leicester's Geordan Murphy has never played for an Irish region because he went to college in England and stayed there. Recently, Tommy Bowe's signing for the Ospreys is the only clear-cut case of an international player being lured out of Ireland. It speaks volumes. No wonder then that the provinces have had continuity to develop and have proved such successes since the introduction of regionalisation in 2003/04. Very rarely do players move from province to province within Ireland either, and most of the development squad for each province come from the locality as well. The obvious exceptions are the players who go to Connacht as part of their induction to the professional game, only to return to their home province afterwards.

The occasional conflict which does arise in Ireland between the IRFU and the provinces is far better than the constant insecurity of the Welsh system. Here, the regions are self-financing and are, therefore, at the mercy of whoever can afford to pay large sums. The WRU does contribute a little, but it's the regions who have to pay their international players. We are extremely lucky at the Scarlets to have four benefactors who have contributed substantially to the club. It started with businessman Huw Evans' financial backing of the club. He founded and is chairman of software group Malborough Sterling. He's been joined more recently by Philip Davies, Tim Griffiths and Glan Wise. All four are very successful businessmen, but each one's support, not just financially but emotionally, in good times and bad, has been an inspiration to me, as it has, I'm sure, to everyone else involved with the Scarlets. In addition to this, there are the long-term sponsors, local companies such as WRW, Dyfed Steel, Gravells and Castell Howell. Within the current system, the Scarlets have been extremely fortunate to get such significant backing. But, on a broader level, the Welsh regions have been left at the mercy of such benefactors to fund their rugby and pay players' wages and, ultimately, to keep them in Wales. At times, it's a case of which regions have the deepest pockets and quite often rugby doesn't come into the picture at all.

13

Captain Scarlet and Some Exits

BACK ON THE field of play we did well in that first season as the Scarlets region, being crowned league champions. We played good rugby and lost very few games. Things were going in the right direction in terms of building the team and developing our style. I had a good end to that first season as well, as coach Gareth Jenkins called me into his office and offered me the captaincy for the forthcoming season. There had been no talk beforehand, so I didn't see it coming and I was delighted to be given such an honour. Stephen Jones had just left the club to go to play in France, so it might well have been a choice between me and him for the captaincy. I recalled missing out on that opportunity to be captain of the first team at Ampleforth, but, on reflection, my leadership skills actually developed later in life anyway. Perhaps my school coach was right after all.

I'd become more and more comfortable as a professional player by the time Gareth asked me to be captain. I felt at ease with my role on the pitch and with my place at the club. When I was asked, I wanted to know if he thought I had the respect of the players. He was convinced that I did. I then shared my thoughts about captaining the side and said that I wasn't the type who would talk incessantly. I would be a captain of few words – I'm not sure if my fellow players would agree with that now, but that's what I thought my style was! I wanted to be a captain who wouldn't expect a player to do anything that I wouldn't do myself – in essence I wanted to lead by example. I knew I wouldn't have to voice big, motivational speeches in the dressing rooms to get the players going. After all, I had rugby's main Mr Motivator himself, Gareth, by my side as coach. He would deal with the dressing room and I would implement what he said on the pitch. A captain's actions should speak louder than his words.

During my first season as captain we reached the final of the EDF Anglo Welsh Cup. We put in a very good performance against Bath in the semi-final, coming from quite a way behind to win 27–26 in the end, with a performance that showed a lot of character. We played Wasps in the final at Twickenham and I was up against my old school contemporary, Lawrence Dallaglio. We were playing well, and Barry Davies had scored a superb try. But, not that long into the first half, I went in to tackle van Gisbergen, and put my head in the wrong position to do so properly. (I wouldn't be too happy about that now as a defence coach!) As a result, I was knocked out cold, falling like a stone to the ground and lying there motionless. I don't actually remember much about the game or the incident, only what I've seen back on television since. I learned from my good friend, Scarlets and Wales winger, Mark Jones, that play carried on for a while after I was knocked out, and that he clearly remembers Dallaglio and several other Wasps players looking at me and carrying on to the next phase of play. Mark, however, realised the severity of the situation and came to my aid while the game carried on. He put me in the recovery position and did what he had to until the medics were allowed on. I was then stretchered off. It must have been the longest first half in rugby history, as Johnny O'Connor, the open-side Irish flanker who played for Wasps, was also seriously injured just before me. The stoppage for his injury was over 15 minutes, as was mine. So, the first half went on for well over an hour.

While I was being treated, Sarra was outside the medical room listening to the panic – I still hadn't come around. All she could hear was our doctor John Martin ask if I could feel anything, with no response coming from me. She said it was one of the worst moments of her life, until she heard me utter the words, "What's the score?" Mum and Dad and Sarra's parents were also very anxious, but coming back to sit on the subs' bench served its purpose. They knew I was OK. Unfortunately, we lost the game in the end. Afterwards, I remember telling Mark off for coming to my aid while the play was still going on – after all, they could have scored a try when he was seeing to me. He replied that there was more to life than conceding a try! It only emerged later how lucky I'd been that Mark had helped me and that I'd actually recovered. Mentioning no names, one or two of the Wasps players could have helped me a little bit sooner.

It would have been a nice start to my captaincy to win a final like that. It was the first year of that new cup competition, where the English and Welsh regions competed against each other. This new cup competition had once been the English Powergen Cup; prior to that the Pilkington Cup and the John Player Cup. The EDF Energy Cup was the first to include the Welsh regions. We did well to get to the final in its first year. In this competition, all Welsh regions have got to at least the semis, with Cardiff and the Opsreys winning it once each. In its first six years, it's 4–2 to the English clubs!

We had lost a few of our more experienced players before that 2005/06 season, those 'go-to' players that you need to turn to when things aren't quite going to plan. Scott Quinell had left, as had Stephen, Salesi Finau and a few of our meatier forwards: Chris Wyatt, Luke Gross and Dave Hodges. So, we had to adopt a different approach to our rugby; there was a shift of emphasis. Some of the physicality had gone from our squad, so we expanded again to our open rugby, with scrum-half Dwayne Peel central to that style, as were Barry Davies and Matthew J Watkins. Gareth Bowen was our outside-half and while a lot of these boys weren't seasoned internationals, we were a team that played well together. We had to change our ways as we had no big ball carriers, no big gain-liners. We had lost the backbone of our squad in 2004/05 and then a few more in 2005/06. But we were consolidating in other ways.

Finally, and not before time, Gareth Jenkins was asked to coach the Welsh team and he took his assistant at Llanelli, Nigel Davies, with him. A vacancy arose, and who should fill it but my former coach at Leeds, Phil Davies! I was really glad to be able to welcome him to Stradey Park, where he had enjoyed such success as a player. I remember speaking to Phil on the phone before he arrived, sharing my enthusiasm for his return. I was delighted that he was coming back, having been away for ten years building Leeds into a Premiership team who had also won the Powergen Cup in 2005. He was leaving Leeds Tykes on a high, and had been away long enough from the Scarlets to have earned his right to coach at the highest level. Therefore, when Gareth Jenkins and Nigel Davies were asked to take over the Welsh national side, Phil saw his chance.

He started coaching the Scarlets in 2006/07. One of his first actions was to bring Stephen Jones back from France. That was a big achievement for Phil, right at the start. There wasn't much he could do as far as the other players were concerned, as he was inheriting players already contracted for that first season.

I was, by then, good friends with Stephen, and I had picked up the vibes that he wasn't totally happy at Clermont. He loved the rugby, and his time there had been successful for him personally, even though the team hadn't won anything. But, the travelling back and forth to Wales was getting him down. Clermont wasn't an easy place to get to, and it meant catching more than one plane, which sometimes included a change at Schipol in Holland! That kind of travelling can be tiring, especially after two years of it. A lot was expected of Steve out there too because he'd gone over there as a marquee player and they really wanted their pound of flesh. Again, this is an example of the better set-up in Ireland – if he'd been an Irish international, he would not have been expected to go back to his region during an international weekend off, but Steve had to go back to France at every possible opportunity.

Stephen and I spoke on the phone about where he

would like to go next. It was obvious that he was thinking in terms of coming back to Wales certainly, but to which club? At about the same time that I was in contact with Steve, separate conversations with Phil made me realise that he was keen to bring Steve back to Llanelli. Both lines of communication were, in essence, made independently of each other but there was an obvious connection to be made. I told both men that I'd love to have Steve back at Stradey. One night Steve and I spoke on the phone for a couple of hours and we had a good, thorough, open chat. I told him of the situation at the club and how things were developing. He listened intently and shared his thoughts, how it would be good to come back, but was that actually the best move? Doubts and fears were honestly discussed.

Stephen then rang me back a few days later to say that Cardiff were interested in signing him and had offered him a contract and he was thinking of signing it. My reply was straightforward. I said, basically, that I respected his decision but I thought it was the wrong one! At this stage, Phil was happy for me to carry on speaking to Steve in order to keep the pressure on him. I hoped that I'd had some influence. Huw Evans and Stuart Gallagher then flew out to France to see Steve personally, to try to persuade him that things were happening at the Scarlets and that Steve needed to be a part of it. In the end, he turned Cardiff down and came back to us, thank goodness.

In that first season, with Phil's coaching and Steve back in the team, we reached the semis of the European Cup again. Phil and Steve built on all that had been started at the club in recent years. Steve's return had an effect on my captaincy as well, because I felt I could now be a little freer, knowing that I had someone of Steve's calibre to turn to, if necessary. He was made vice-captain – not a bad vice-captain to have! We had a nucleus of players to build a team around forwards Iestyn Thomas and Matthew Rees and backs Mark Jones and Regan King. It was an exciting time, as footballing prowess started to take over, instead of the forward power of my first few years at the Scarlets. We beat London Irish away, 32–25, probably one of the best games I've ever been involved in, because of the new style of our play. Mark Jones scored a great individual try and I scored one as well, one of my very few! We secured maximum points having scored four tries as a team. We then beat Ulster at home 21–15, followed by a 21–19 victory over Toulouse at Stradey. Unfortunately, both myself and Mark Jones missed the away game because we were both injured. We watched the game together at my house and by half-time, we were both suicidal as the Scarlets were way behind, down 24–3 and then 31–10. But, by the end of the game we were like two crazy children, dancing and rejoicing at what had been one of the great comebacks in a classic European game. We'd turned it around and won 34–41. Adrenalin had dissolved our injuries momentarily, and we were just *so* proud of the boys. We had London Irish, Ulster and Toulouse in our European group and we got to the end of the group stages undefeated, in what was undoubtedly, the group of death! That doesn't happen very often!

Next up in the quarter-finals were the then European champions, Munster, the team representing the region of my grandmother's family on my mother's side. I feel an affinity to Munster, more than to any other province. They're one team that I would have enjoyed playing for, but never got the opportunity. Having said that, it would be difficult to break into a back-row that consisted of Quinlan, Wallace and Foley! I think that the Scarlets have an affinity with Munster too. Both are very similar regions, due to their geographical positions in their respective countries. Both have similar working-class roots and community spirit. They are two regions that mirror each other, and one playing the other that day in such a high-profile competition was quite special. Winning was obviously a good feeling.

Not only were we going back to the old ways on the pitch, but Phil also started a pre-match tradition that, in my mind, really worked. He started asking former Scarlets legends to come to the dressing room before each game, and to hand out the shirts to each player. These former players emphasised that we were really just *custodians* of those shirts – we didn't own them. We wore them to continue the tradition and we were not to disappoint those who had worn the shirts before us. Jonathan Davies came, as did Ieuan Evans, Phil Bennet and Delme Thomas, amongst others. It was something very special to us and made us feel connected to a long line of Scarlets players as they told us what it had meant for them to wear that same shirt. Prior to that, the legendary Ray Gravell used to come into the dressing room before each game. We never tired of Grav's infectious enthusiasm as he spoke to us passionately before matches and got us whipped-up before taking to the pitch, making us feel as though we could take anyone on.

But, by the time we beat Munster convincingly, and headed for the semi-finals, Grav had been hospitalised and had had his leg amputated below the knee as a result of diabetes.

On the morning of our European Cup semi-final against, yes, Leicester again, at the Walker Stadium, Grav phoned me from his hospital bed, emotional as ever, and wished us all the best for the match. I really appreciated that call and it felt as if he was there with us that day. Another story linked with Grav and that particular game was the one about the hospital authorities arranging to get Sky TV in his private room on the ward, so that Grav could watch the Scarlets v Leicester game. But, Grav was adamant that he didn't want such an arrangement. If no one else could watch Sky on the ward, why should he – why do this just for him and for no one else? So Grav listened to the game on the radio. What a man! One special feature of that match day was the hundreds of banners and rugby shirts wishing Grav all the best. It was a clear sign of how much he was loved.

What he heard on the radio was probably not to his entire satisfaction unfortunately. Just as in the game against Leicester at Welford Road in 2001/02, we started well. We went ahead in the game, we then went behind, but we then went ahead again, only to lose by a fair margin in the end.

After that Leicester game, I went through a period of questioning myself in a way that I hadn't done before. I was plagued by doubts about my own ability as captain. Why couldn't I inspire the team more? Why did we throw away a lead under my captaincy? Did I have the right influence on my team-mates? Why couldn't I take my team to the final stage of a competition it had never been to before? Loads of different questions were going round and round in my head. We stopped at the Belfry on the way back from Leicester, which we had planned to do, win or lose, and I shared my doubts with Phil. I also spoke to Steve and Mark Jones. I knew the three well enough to know that they would not say what I wanted to hear, but that they'd tell me the truth. Thankfully they all backed me up. But going through such a process was a new experience for me.

That was in April and, not long after, I was asked to be the captain for the following season as well, my third at the helm. That was quite a vote of confidence. It turned out, however, to be quite a stormy season! We were doing well as a club and, again, creating a lot of interest. We were in a good position to sign new players as we would have been an attractive proposition for any quality rugby player. We probably only needed two or three marquee players which would have been enough to consolidate our squad and take us to the holy grail, the European Cup.

It was also a World Cup year, so many of our players were likely to be away for a couple of months. Key areas needed to be covered therefore, and Phil decided that the best approach was not to sign just two or three class players but seven or eight good players. I think the logic was that six or seven of us would be away for the World Cup and the best course of action to fill those gaps would be these new signings. We had, therefore, players who could do a job and sustain us for the period during which the squad would be without its World Cup internationals. But the players the club signed didn't stay more than two years. At the time, we really could have signed who we wanted, and secured players who could have been a part of the long-term structure and development of the club. It really was an opportunity missed to take us on to the next level. I don't think that the two or three world-class players needed would have cost more than the seven or eight we actually got. But those two or three could well have been a better investment. It was also a shame that we lost two of our key players, Barry Davies and Matthew J Watkins – Matthew being told that he was no longer a part of the plan at Stradey.

When I returned from the World Cup, things were different at the Scarlets. At most clubs there are some players who aren't happy for different reasons but, at Stradey then, the whole squad seemed to have issues. The biggest problem, and the one which caused the most unrest, was the conditioning regime that was introduced. On that level it was felt that things were turning into a dictatorship.

Phil brought in a guy called Adam Carey, a highly-qualified nutritionist who had worked with Olympic teams and the England rugby team, to name but two. Unfortunately, his methods and his approach affected the morale of the squad. He was telling players some blunt facts to their faces, such as that they were too fat, but without getting to know them first and earning their respect. He came across as being way too heavy-handed. His aim was to get us all down to our minimum weight and make us as lean as possible. Some players went from about 105 kg to 90 kg in a couple of months. The idea, then, was to build us back up from there. For me, rugby is about different shapes and sizes. What we lacked at the club, at that time, were those big, bulky players with physical presence who were awkward to budge. For me, Adam Carey was an outsider who was trying to change things in an unconstructive way. This approach significantly added to the general unrest.

As captain, I was very much aware of the way the

players felt. But also, knowing Phil the way I do, I knew that everything he was putting in place was what he thought was best for the club and the players to move us forward. On a personal level, where would I have been without Phil phoning me up, a farm hand on his tractor, and offering a professional rugby contract? That opportunity and the support, enthusiasm and advice over the following years had put me on the road to being an international rugby player. But I couldn't be blind to what was happening around me at the Scarlets at the time. I also had my responsibility as a captain to the team.

Meetings were held between the players, Phil, Wayne Proctor and management to try and sort things out. But things were still sour.

Then a headline in the *Western Mail* newspaper took the troubles at the Scarlets to another level. Some of us arrived at work one morning having seen a story in the paper that Phil had been sacked. I went to see him straightaway, and he knew nothing about it. As far as he was concerned, it was business as usual. But, the *Western Mail* had obviously got the story from somewhere. It was upsetting for all involved that the press knew first.

By lunchtime the whole squad had been called to a meeting and were told that Phil was being relieved of his duties. As uneasy as things had been of late, the players were genuinely disappointed and shocked that things had come to a head like this. I was gutted for Phil. Our complaints hadn't meant that we wanted a change at the top. The players just wanted to be heard; they wanted to try to solve the issues together and move on.

About a week later, it was confirmed that Nigel Davies would return to the club to be head coach the following season. I knew Nigel very well from my first few years as a Scarlet. Again, like Phil, Nigel was a passionate Scarlet with a vision of how he wanted to move us forward. We were heading into a brand new season and Nigel asked me to remain as captain. I wasn't sure at first because the club had obviously decided to move away from Phil's leadership, and maybe it was time for somebody else to take on the captain's role as well. After talking in depth with Nigel about his aspirations for the club, I accepted the captaincy and looked forward with excitement to a new chapter in the club's history.

14

Ireland! Ireland!

WHAT A FEELING it was to get that first invitation to play for my country! I'd turned down Clive Woodward's call to play for England. I'd signed for a region that would increase my chance of catching the Irish selectors' eye. When I signed for the Scarlets, I knew that they had Ulster in their Heineken Cup group that season and that would put me right up there as far as the 'Irish shop window' was concerned. And thankfully, it paid off.

Two members of the Irish coaching set-up under Warren Gatland were sent to watch me play. Eddie O'Sullivan and Donal Lenihan came up to see me play at Ravenhill, when the Scarlets were playing against the then European champions, Ulster. They had won the European Cup the previous year, before the English teams entered the competition. At Ravenhill, it was a wet, windy and horrible game, so it gave me a chance to be quite effective! The Scarlets won and I gave a good performance in front of the Irish coaches.

Come the Six Nations then, both Guy and I were selected to play for Ireland A – the first game being against England A in Northampton on the Friday night before England played Ireland at Twickenham. It was a good game because, not only did we win, but both Guy and I scored tries. Tim Stimpson missed a last-minute kick that would have given England victory, so it was 27–26 to us.

The following day, Guy and I were back in Cardiff, enjoying our call-up to the Ireland A team, scoring a try each and beating England A. But, our joy was short lived, as we watched the England v Ireland game on TV on the Saturday afternoon. Ireland were stuffed! I felt a whole host of mixed emotions at the heavy loss. I felt gutted at first, but then, in the back of my mind, I began to think about the possibilities for me as an individual player. It was a strange dual feeling, pulling in two different directions. Could this awful result actually be my big chance? All the commentators analysing the match said that changes needed to be made. Could I be part of that change?

On Sunday morning, the call came. I was asked to be part of the 35-man Ireland squad, and had the opportunity to be part of the Irish senior side in the next game against Scotland. What a feeling! A few minutes later, I heard that Guy had been called up as well. Wholesale changes had been made: Ronan O'Gara, Frankie Sheahan and Peter Stringer were already in the squad but hadn't played for Ireland yet, and Shane Horgan and John Hayes were also called up at the same time as Guy and me. So, we made the trip over to Ireland to be a part of the training camp. There was a two-week gap before the Scotland game; so it was training for a few days in the first week, then another regroup at the beginning of the actual match week.

The crucial day was the Tuesday before the game at

the weekend. That morning we learned if we were part of the match squad or not. If we weren't, it was back to our club, region or province. So, it was an anxious wait that morning. I waited in the same room as people who I'd admired for a long time, players such as: Keith Wood, Victor Costello, Kevin Maggs, the exciting new talent that was Brian O'Driscoll and so many others. My mind filled with thoughts that I could be named on the same team sheet as these top players. When my name did get called out, I didn't hear anyone else's name mentioned at all! I heard my name and then completely switched off, lost in the moment. Five of us made our debuts in that game, Ronan at 10, Peter Stringer at 9, Shane on the wing, John at prop as well as me. Now, looking back, the five of us have over 400 caps, with Ronan and John crossing the hundred-cap mark. That wasn't a bad selection at all on Warren Gatland's part! Guy was also selected for the bench, so he would be part of the set-up on match day with me. That was quite special and was the cause of much celebration in the Easterby household.

After the selection, I was on quite a high and keen to justify my selection in the training session afterwards. But, it is such a temptation to over do it. There's a saying in rugby that if you train like Tarzan you'll probably play like Jane! I most certainly didn't want to fall into that trap. I tried my best to train as if I hadn't been selected. Gat's approach to training concentrated on the physical aspect, as it still does. He's told me since that he knew that I'd played well for Ireland A against England A, but the clincher for him was the way I trained. This year Gatland took some Welsh players who he wouldn't necessarily have seen in a match situation to the World Cup. They'd obviously impressed him in training sessions.

My selection for the Ireland team also closed the chapter in terms of turning down the chance to play for England. My decision had now been justified. It helped enormously that I'd come to a region where things were happening and that had boosted my cause no end. I was extremely pleased to get the chance to play for my country so soon after leaving Leeds and turning England down. A lot can happen in six months.

As match day, the 19th of February 2000, approached, we were all staying in the Glen View Hotel in Greystones, near Bray, just outside Dublin. On the Thursday, we trained on an adjacent pitch at Lansdowne Road and then moved into the Berkley Court Hotel on Lansdowne Road itself. From that Thursday on, you went into match day mode. Moving to the Berkley Court Hotel certainly intensified that feeling because you could see the stadium, where you were to get your first cap, from the hotel. An occasional glance in that direction in the day or two before the match would focus your thoughts on what was ahead.

The captain's talk before dinner on the Friday night was quite stirring. Keith Wood captained the side then, and he told us simply, but powerfully, what was expected of us on the pitch the following day. It was, for me, quite something to be captained by Woody. It was an honour to sit there listening to such an inspirational character and a world-class rugby player.

Another real character played a central role in the preparation of the Irish squad prior to matches. Rala is an institution in his own right! Paddy O'Reilly is Rala's real name, and he has been the kit-man for Ireland for years. He's a one-off, an eccentric, but someone you could call upon for a pint or for advice on a personal matter. Rala always needed a suite at any hotel because he wanted space to lay out all the kit he had for us. He'd line up our shorts and socks, everything we'd need to clean our boots, and anything else from a spare belt to toothpaste. He was the original *Open All Hours* Arkwright store!

As a result, most of the lads would spend their Friday night down time in and out of Rala's suite, just relaxing, watching TV or chatting. It seemed quite low key, but it was an integral part of the pre-match routine, and had grown into a ritual. Rala was also at the receiving end of a few players' pranks as well, usually instigated by Peter Stringer and John Hayes, with Peter being the brains behind any escapade and John being the enforcer! It was all part of team building of course! Once, we strapped him to a luggage trolley in a hotel, gagged him and sent him down in the lift to the foyer, wearing nothing more than a pair of Y-fronts! But, he plays a key role in the Irish set-up and does to this day, and he did for me that night before my first cap. It certainly was a help to chill out in such an atmosphere and I'm glad that I wasn't sitting in a room on my own for most of the night. I shared a room with Keiron Dawson who was to play Number 7 against Scotland, with me at Number 6. All teams need glue to hold them together. For a long time at Llanelli, we've had Wayne 'Wayno' James who is our Rala – always there for us as players and management.

The morning of the match arrived and I opened the curtains of the bedroom and looked out onto Lansdowne Road and saw that some people were already beginning to mill around. Down in the foyer, fans wearing their rugby shirts were beginning to turn up. The atmosphere was slowly building – you could feel it. There was no way that we would get that buzz if we'd stayed a distance from the ground. Personally, I found it to be a great help to be right in the thick of it and wake up in Lansdowne Road. After breakfast, we had a few line-out practices, nothing too strenuous, and while the forwards would do some work, the backs would chat!

After lunch, there was a team meeting and then we made our way onto the team bus. The hotel foyer was packed with fans as we walked to the bus, and walking through that sea of noise was amazing. As I was to find out amazing, that seemed to be a feature of all Irish internationals, wherever we played. Realising on the day of my first game that so many fans just turn up to see us get on the bus, certainly made me feel ten feet tall.

As you walk out of the Barclay Court Hotel, the Lansdowne Road stadium is only about 150 metres away. However, another Irish ritual is that we go on a mile-and-a-half team bus journey to get to the stadium! This does two things. It lets players settle on the bus while, at the same time, allowing players to take in a bit of the atmosphere that's building up in the city as we pass all the pubs on the way, the cheering fans and cars beeping their horns. That's when it hit me that I was playing more than just a rugby match – I was playing for my country, for all these people we passed on the streets. The only other bus journey which would be anywhere near as exciting is the one to the stadium in Paris. Those journeys would be under police escort, with police whistles blowing incessantly as they got the team bus to the Stade de France in record time.

After arriving at the stadium it was a matter of trying to ease away from all that build-up and start thinking more about the rugby in hand. Then your usual match-day routine kicked in. That is, until you walked out of the tunnel. The roar was like nothing I'd ever heard. The intensity that had been building up from the moment I opened the curtains in the hotel had just reached another new level altogether. And it was to go up another notch again as we stood for the anthems. I had a rough idea where mum and dad and my sister sat and, as luck would have it, I saw them in the stand and we made eye contact. To add to that, I was standing, linking arms with my brother. We both stood singing the anthem side by side, with our parents and sister looking on. You just can't describe that feeling. Different things were going through your mind, but the overriding thought was why I was there in the first place. Thoughts of my mum and her parents and the Irish heritage swelled up inside me as the anthem rang around Lansdowne. Pride is a powerful emotion.

After all that, it was off with the tracksuit to play the biggest game of rugby you've ever played in your life! You have to manage the occasion and produce a performance. That's international rugby. That first blow of the ref's whistle kicks you into autopilot and everything else by then has been put to one side as the rugby takes over.

That's how I felt in the run-up to my first cap. The buzz of that first day never left me; I felt that excitement every time I took to the pitch for Ireland. In fact, I think I've got more emotional as I've grown older. Certain matches give you more of a buzz than others, such as when I played England for the first time at Twickenham and when Guy and I played together for the first time. But not in one game did I lose that sense of playing for my country and what that meant.

Playing against team-mates was to be another new

rugby experience too as, four weeks after that first game, we played Wales in Dublin. Two of the Scarlets lads, Stephen Jones and Rupert Moon, were in the Welsh team. Steve and I had become good friends and there was nervous and apprehensive texting between us in the week leading up to the game. I don't think either of us wished the other good luck; it was more of a case of low-key banter. To make matters worse, Moonie had a really good game and got the Man of the Match award as Wales beat us 23–19. The Wales games have always been special ever since.

After that first game, which we won comfortably 44–22, it was time to enjoy being an international player back at the Barclay Court Hotel – but not too much of course, as we were in the middle of a Six Nations campaign. All new players get toasted by their team-mates and the opposition, which is nice. Luckily, they didn't give me too difficult a time, choosing as they did to pick more on Shane, John and Ronan.

I was still on a high well into Sunday. In those days, I read the newspaper reports because I believed that rugby correspondents knew more about the game than they actually did, and took their word as gospel. I had good reports that day, which confirmed my view! I went out for a celebration lunch with my family on Sunday. But, by Sunday night, I still wasn't sure what Gats thought of my game and, being new to the situation, I didn't know what the procedure was in that squad set-up for feedback. Anyway, come Sunday night at about 8 p.m., I got a call from team manager, Brian O'Brian, to go and see Gats and himself for a chat. Into the room I went, and Gats asked me:

"Did you have a good time yesterday?"

"Yes, great thanks, I really enjoyed the match."

"Did you enjoy last night?"

"Yes, great, had a good time with the lads, thanks."

"OK, have a look at this video recording Simon. But before we see it, have you got anything you want to say?"

I said that I hadn't and carried on thinking that this was going to be the analysis of my game and looked forward to the chance to discuss it with the coach. But what I saw was CCTV footage of someone walking through the hotel lobby and into the bar – stark naked!

"Have you got anything to say now?"

Foolishly, I thought that humour might help.

"He's in good condition, whoever he is!"

They didn't laugh. I had gone into the toilet that night, taken off all my clothes, folded them neatly under my arm, and walked naked through the packed hotel lobby into the bar. There, I'd ordered a drink and had a conversation with the president of the Irish Rugby Football Union. Then I'd rejoined the lads, again as nature intended. Later, I also learned that a little further along the bar, Brian O'Driscoll was standing with his trousers and underpants around his ankles. But the CCTV didn't pick that up, and it was me stood in front of the boss. He then asked me:

"Is this you?"

"Mmm, I don't know, looks more like my brother to me and it's the sort of thing he'd do."

"He's already said that about you!" was Gats' instant reply.

I didn't know that they'd already spoken to Guy and, after he'd left them, he'd tried to contact me to warn me about what was to happen. I apologised to them both and was told firmly that it was not to happen again. I am so lucky that all this happened years ago – otherwise if it had happened now, the recording would be all over YouTube, with stills in the newspapers. I avoided all that sensationalism, thank goodness.

I walked out of the room with my head down. As disciplined as Gats and Brian were that day, I later learned from both of them that they were absolutely in hysterics when they first saw the video and had a real good laugh. But, they couldn't show me that on the day, which is fair enough.

No doubt, I was on a massive high during the weekend of my first cap. But, because of that one incident, I could well have been a one-cap wonder. Thank Gats that I wasn't!

15

With Ireland on the World Stage

I ARRIVED AT Llanelli in 1999, the World Cup year, and the competition was being held in Wales. Therefore, I got to experience a great deal of the World Cup set-up and atmosphere, and the Welsh boys in the Scarlets squad shared with me how they felt about it all. But as good as that was, nothing actually beats taking part in a World Cup itself. That was my next ambition once I was established in the Irish team.

The irony was that, when the next World Cup came along, I wasn't a guaranteed selection for the Irish team. I had slipped back a bit – to the A team in the previous season, but thankfully, was still part of the squad. So the pre-World Cup tour to Australia, Tonga and Samoa was even more crucial for me. Good performances there were essential if I was to savour experiencing my first World Cup. I hadn't held a regular place in the previous Six Nations, and it was the Ireland side which ended that campaign which played the first match of the tour against the Aussies in Perth. Those of us who weren't an automatic first choice would make up the bulk of the squad going on to Tonga and Samoa. Basically, that's where we had to prove ourselves and play for our places. We were either coming back to that corner of the world in a few months time for the World Cup or staying at home and playing for our clubs.

We all watched the first team play Australia in Perth. Then the senior players flew home and we went further on, to the South Sea Islands. Not even a year in Australia had prepared me for the weather that we experienced in Tonga. It was horrendously hot, dry and humid. Some of the boys got sunstroke during matches. It was an alien environment for us but one that brought out the best in us, and we thrived on it. We didn't really get the best of starts in Tonga, either. Our hotel, the Dateline, was only half built and they were working through the night to get it finished! Sleep was an optional extra therefore, but we soon got used to it and really enjoyed our time in Tonga. We beat their national team, before moving on to Samoa for a week.

America has had more of an influence on Samoa, so it was a little bit more modern. We won our game there as well. Both games had gone well for me, so I headed home knowing that I had at least done what was expected of me – I was sure I was a contender for selection.

That selection wasn't secured until after a few months of training in the summer. After the Tonga and Samoa tour, we had a weekend off before a final camp in Bilbao, Spain. I was able to see my girlfriend, Sarra, a TV presenter, who is the daughter of Wales and British Lion winger, Elgan Rees. She was in Manchester working on a children's TV programme. The deal, as far as the Irish management was concerned, was that if you didn't receive a phone call by a certain cut-off time, then you'd been selected for the World Cup squad. That time came and went without the phone ringing. I was in! I made a quick phone call to double check, and then I let it sink in slowly – I was going to the premier rugby competition in the world. As a result of a combination of my long-term injuries and also other players coming in to the squad and playing well and keeping their places, I'd been out of the Ireland team for almost two years. This moment, therefore, was one to savour.

We had a good team going to that World Cup in Australia. Keith Wood was coming to the end of his career and wanted to lead his country in a successful World Cup campaign. We left Ireland with a fair amount of hope for a good run. We had a tough group though: Australia and, for a second World Cup in a row, Argentina as well as Namibia and Romania. We beat those last two countries easily, before moving on to play Argentina in Adelaide.

The Argentina game was, without doubt, one of the toughest games I've ever played in because of what was at stake. Both teams knew that a victory would mean a first or second place in the group, with Australia to be played next for us. I had two reasons to be excited about the Argentina game. I'd managed to work myself back into the team and we were to play them at the Adelaide Oval. Guy and I were overwhelmed to play on such a hallowed cricket ground. It is legendary in cricketing history; it's the place where Lance Gibbs took the first ever Test match hat-trick; the first ever cricket one-day International was held there, and in the early '90s the ground witnessed the narrowest Test defeat ever, when the West Indies beat Australia by one run. Playing there meant so much more to me because I was an avid cricket fan too.

One other World Cup game was played there – Australia beat Namibia 142–0! We didn't achieve that kind of score. Our margin of victory was a little closer, 16–15. But it was a win and it set up our next match against Australia in Melbourne for the pool decider. Would it be Australia or us going to the quarter-finals as pool winners? It was another game won by the narrowest possible margin, 17–16 to Australia, after a late David Humphreys drop-goal attempt went narrowly wide. Despite that, we felt that we had played well, had proven our ability as a team and that the World Cup was going OK for us. But, that changed in the next game against France, the quarter-final game. We did the one thing which you can't do against any French team – we gave them a chance to accrue lots of points on the board early on. I think they were about 20 points up in the first 25 minutes. The stuffing was knocked out of us and we lost 43–21 eventually. I think that the Argentina and Australia games had taken a lot out of us and we might have run out of steam by the time we faced France. We could see the semi-finals on the horizon and a chance to take Ireland further than they'd been before in the competition. But, we fell just short. It was disappointing, no doubt, but not a disgrace.

After many months preparing for and playing in the World Cup, we were finally able to let our hair down after the quarter-final loss. Melbourne has a large casino, and Frankie Sheahan, the Munster hooker who was number two to Keith Wood, fancied his chances. He arrived late at the casino table, sat next to Anthony

Foley and started playing. He couldn't believe his eyes when he saw the first hand he'd been dealt. It was a royal flush! The jackpot was his therefore, a staggering A$90,000! Frankie thought he could keep the amount he'd won quiet. He tried for a few days, afraid that the management might not approve. There was no issue, as it happens, but it was fun making sure that Frankie had to buy our secrecy for as long as possible. The drinks were certainly on him that night – and a few other nights too.

I managed to take a short holiday after Ireland were knocked out. Sarra had travelled out to Australia with some other players' wives and partners, so Guy, Kevin Maggs and his wife Jane, and Sarra and I spent a few days together. That was nice, as I was able to show Sarra some of the places that were special to me when I lived in Sydney. I also met up with some old friends, including Andrew McInnerney. We also managed to meet up with Stephen Jones for a while, driving up to the northern beaches for a few days when his duties with Wales were over. I began to put the strains of the World Cup behind me before flying home.

If we had a great deal of hope going into the 2003 World Cup, we had real aspirations going into the 2007 tournament. We felt that the last four, if not the final, was within our grasp. We went into that World Cup off the back of a very successful Six Nations tournament, losing out on the title to France by the narrowest of margins. We beat Wales in Cardiff, England in Dublin (but more on that game later) and Scotland at Murrayfield. We scored over 150 points in those matches, but the final table placing shows that we were second because of two very late tries. One of those was against us in the Italy match which reduced our points difference, and the other was for France against Scotland, which increased theirs. There's no sour grapes at all on my part, but, the French try was awarded as a result of a rather dubious decision by the video referee. So we lost out on the Six Nations title by points difference only.

However, that still put us in good spirits for the World Cup. We knew we had a great team. We knew we could perform at the highest level. There was a confidence and a buoyant mood in the Irish camp going to France for that year's World Cup.

In 2003, our base for the World Cup had been in a coastal area north of Sydney. It was a really nice environment; we all stayed together and everything was on hand. There was a small town within easy walking distance where we could enjoy the down time, and the beach was good for unwinding after training sessions. All this helped break up the monotony of being in a camp situation.

But, in 2007, we were just off the motorway and near a man-made lake in an enterprise park, about 30 minutes taxi ride from Bordeaux! It could not have been more different to the previous tournament's base. That was not a good start for us and, as loathe as I am to put any blame on the conditions where we stayed for our disappointing performance on the pitch, there is absolutely no doubt that our day-to-day comfort was a big factor during our time in France. We were isolated there, almost trapped, to be honest. I think many of us went a little bit stir-crazy in such an environment. The discontent increased the longer we stayed there. A few players would voice this off-record to some of the press, but it didn't stay off-record for long. It certainly helped fill column inches in the wall-to-wall press coverage the World Cup gets.

At the time social media, such as Facebook, was becoming more and more popular. Someone, outside the Irish squad, decided to put a story on Facebook saying that Geordan Murphy had gone missing from the Irish camp. Messages such as, 'Where's Geordan gone?' started to appear on the site. Against the backdrop of existing discontent, the press loved this story and also started printing the 'Geordan's gone AWOL' line. I first learned about this when the guy I was sharing a room with on that campaign read it out to me. And that guy was Geordan Murphy!

It would have been a funny one-off at any other time. But in this context, it just made things a lot worse. The bad-feeling stories escalated after that. The press were convinced that there were other issues underlying this general discontent at our base. Mostly they got it wrong. But it would be unfair to say that our accommodation was the main source of the problem.

Other problems came to the surface too once we'd played our first matches. We were expected to beat both Georgia and Namibia quite comfortably in the group stages, especially after the way we'd played at the end of the Six Nations. We did win both games, but not as convincingly as we were expected to. We beat Namibia 32–17, a scoreline which flatters, and Georgia by 14–10 which was as bad as it looks.

Now the questions were flying at us. What's wrong? What's wrong with your camp? Is it problems in the squad? Is it a problem with Eddie O'Sullivan? Do the players have a problem with each other? And on, and on, and on.

Off the pitch, there were issues with the facilities which affected team morale. On the pitch there were also issues, which had nothing to do with our accommodation. It was up to the players to put any off-the-pitch issues behind us as soon as the rugby playing got underway. If we didn't, then it was the players' responsibility. On the pitch, other factors kicked in. Maybe the seeds of discontent for some of those issues *were* to be found in the three warm-up games played before the World Cup. We only just beat Italy, we lost to Scotland and we played a horrendous game against Bayonne (who were just out to maim us as much as they could before the World Cup, or at least that's the impression they gave!). Brian O'Driscoll received a heavy knock to the face and was in real danger of missing the World Cup. It probably wasn't the best idea to play a French team in France before a World Cup in France when France were in your group! So, there were feelings of negativity before we even got to our base.

Having only just managed to defeat Georgia and Namibia, we then had to travel to Paris to play France. They had recently lost to Argentina – who were in our group for the third World Cup in a row – so they were on the back foot and had something to prove. We lost to France as well. We then returned to our base near Bordeaux, which didn't help at all, because we already hated the place. So, having not won as we should have, there wasn't a positive environment to go back to between games to regroup. And one thing just compounded the other.

In our last group game, we needed to beat Argentina, back in Paris, by a margin of over 20 points. We didn't have it in us to do that and our World Cup aspirations were over. It was a huge disappointment.

Looking back on that campaign, it was a case of one factor leading to another and no let-up in the schedule to put things right. Once the matches versus Namibia and Georgia had gone the way they did, the coaching team was in a really difficult position. If we'd have beaten Namibia comfortably, as expected, there would have been significant team changes for the Georgia game. And the team to play France would have been the strongest from those previous two matches. But, with things not going well and the team not performing, it was difficult to change the line-up, as the team needed an opportunity to gain some form. It certainly wasn't an option to make any changes to the team which took on France. As a result, some players didn't get the chance to play at all and that didn't help matters at our base either. We had a squad who were: unhappy with the accommodation arrangements (with the press helping to escalate any discontent); disappointed, as not all was going to plan on the pitch, and with a group of about five or six players who hadn't had the chance to play and felt totally out of it all. And they, to be fair, were in no way trying to undermine the rest of us, but were just voicing their own frustrations and unease, which, although they didn't mean to do so, added to all the negativity.

In a World Cup every squad member should get the opportunity to play at some stage. You're together for such a long time, so to be a part of the set-up and not play any rugby is demoralising. In my playing position of flanker, Alan Quinlan and Steven Ferris didn't get a chance to play even though they should have done. I got selected continuously, but I still felt for those who weren't playing at all. So, maybe the selection for that second game in the World Cup could have been different, and that would have made a difference to team morale. In the 2011 World Cup, Ireland gave everyone an opportunity to play by the time of the third match against Russia. That was good for the squad.

Not one individual element is solely responsible for a disastrous campaign. Our World Cup in 2007 started to fail at the pre-World Cup stage and just got worse from there. This year, Ireland managed to turn around a disappointing run-up to perform well in the tournament itself. And this year, the Irish lads really enjoyed the World Cup away from the pitch. Everything was in place. I'm sure that the senior players, like Ronan O'Gara, Brian O'Driscoll and Paul O'Connell had an input, as they would have remembered only too well the circumstances from 2007. When you're together for a long period of time, in a pressure situation at the top tournament in the world, it's crucial that all the elements are right.

Ireland played really well in the 2011 World Cup. But, in that game against Wales, they did lose to a better team on the day! I would add, though, that Ireland did manage to do something Wales couldn't, which is beat a Tri-Nations team in the southern hemisphere! That was a magnificent achievement. Wales will need to show that they can do that if the obvious success they've had in the World Cup is to be developed upon.

Now that I'm part of the coaching team at the Scarlets, I'm able to welcome back the club's Welsh World Cup stars and work with them in the regional set-up. It's an exciting prospect, as Rhys Priestland, Scott Williams, Jon Davies and George North all shone in New Zealand and Tavis Knoyle and Ken Owens made the most of the opportunities they were given. There's also the slight matter of welcoming back Wales' all-time record cap holder, Stephen Jones! These players certainly benefited from all the preparations they went through before going to New Zealand. I would also like to add, however, that these players didn't develop into World Cup heroes just in the two months before the tournament. The Welsh set-up inherited fit and skilful individuals who'd been developed over a long time by the regions. It's not entirely fair to say that the Welsh national team preparations made all the difference and, in my opinion, not enough attention has been given to how the players attained their levels of fitness and skill in the first place, especially their conditioning. All of the regional fitness coaches feel this has been credited to the Wales coaches only, and that the fact it was a combined effort has largely been overlooked.

To compare Wales and Ireland again, this year's World Cup highlights, once again, the strange situation in the two countries. The Welsh national team are playing very well and are eye-catching on the world stage. But, the Welsh regions have not had the success of the Irish regions at a European level. That's hard to understand. If Wales keep the squad they had this year, they stand a good chance of going into the next World Cup as one of the three or four favourites to win it. Maybe, in the set-up at the Scarlets, with so many players who shone for Wales coming back to us now, we can start to close that gap on the Irish regions. The Scarlets haven't got a bad record in Europe. We've just celebrated winning our 100th European game, more than any other Welsh region, so we have a legacy to draw upon. Now we've got the individual players as well to move us on to the next level.

On a personal note, I found both the World Cups I took part in to be invaluable experiences. There's nothing like that competition because it's a knock-out competition in a tour environment. It's the highest level at which I could represent my country and I'm glad to have been able to do so.

However, once again in my life, but not for anything like the same reason, a major rugby event was overshadowed by a personal story. Mum and dad had decided to come out to watch me play in the World Cup and they had always supported myself and Guy whenever and wherever we played, even managing to be impartial when we played against each other. But now, it was our family's time to support dad. Just before going to France, he had been diagnosed with cancer of the oesophagus. He soon had to decide whether or not to have a major operation to remove the growth. It wasn't an easy decision; there were obviously complications to any major surgery but, with all our backing and support, he decided to go ahead with the surgery. On his return from France he went into hospital. He was laid low by that surgery and was out of action for months. He did manage to get back to do very light duties on the farm, but he found that as difficult to cope with as the illness itself, because he couldn't do as much he used to be able to do.

The Scarlets were away at Connacht in November 2008 when I got a call from Guy saying that dad's cancer had returned. The cancer was in his back now. Guy told me that there was to be no recovery this time. All of a sudden playing rugby in Ireland didn't mean so much.

There were some very difficult times after that. I vowed to travel up to Yorkshire at every opportunity, and the club were amazing in their support with Nigel Davies, in particular, giving me plenty of time off to do so. The time gave me real closure on some of the things that had been lurking in my mind over the years – nothing dramatic, but things that I would have regretted not being able to discuss with dad had I not had the opportunity. I guess it was a case of being able to avoid the 'I wish I could have told him while he was still alive' regret that so many people, maybe men in particular, feel for years after the passing of a parent or a close family member.

Guy, Debs and I spent hours with him, which was a very special time for us as his children but also for us as brothers and sister. We sat for hours around that kitchen table in the house where we'd all grown up and spoke of our childhood memories, shared emotions, discussed our fears and how life would be now without dad. It's funny how a situation of desperation and sadness brings people even closer together, and I remember at that time of adversity, looking around the table at my brother and sister, thinking how much I loved them and how thankful I was that the three of us were there for each other and going through all this together. It was a difficult time for us and our mum watching the man she'd loved slipping away. They had remained close throughout the years and knowing that the father of her children wouldn't be around to be 'papa' to their grandchildren was difficult for her.

Each time I went back to see dad, I could see a marked change. He went from walking around the farm to being housebound, from sitting in a chair and then being bedbound, within a very short space of time. I was in Yorkshire on the day he passed away. I had stayed with him for a few hours during the night and then Guy arrived to take over. I went to get some sleep and Guy later came in to tell me that dad had gone. It was obviously heart wrenching, but I was so glad that dad was no longer in pain. I was also relieved, more than anything else, that I'd had the opportunity to tell him how much I loved him and how proud I was of him. The three of us, in our own way, had told him that we hoped that we too had made him proud. It was a tough time, but it was a special time that will always stay with me.

On the day of the funeral, the village was covered in snow and, walking with dad for the very last time down from the farm to the village church with those snowflakes falling from the sky was something that will stay with me forever. The country had been hit hard by some severe weather, but people still came from all over to pay their respects to dad. Scarlets coach Nigel Davies, Gareth Jenkins, team manager Anthony Buchanan and Scarlets main sponsor and good friend Robert Williams travelled up. I will always appreciate them making that effort to travel so far through the snow to the funeral. The day dad died, Sarra and Soffia were up in Yorkshire with me. So, at the passing of the man who had brought me up, those close to me in the life I had been able to build because of his guidance, support and encouragement, were there with me.

It's very tough to accept that a man you thought was invincible could deteriorate to such an extent. As a son, I had put my dad on a pedestal throughout my life, and it was horrific to see what the illness had done to this fine, proud man. It was even harder to see him being taken away from me.

16

British and Irish

STRADEY PARK, 2005. I was there with some of my team mates, Welsh scrum-half Dwayne Peel, specifically. We were both watching *Sky News* to find out if we'd been selected for the British and Irish Lions tour of New Zealand. It was good news for Dwayne, but not for me. I was gutted. I had high hopes of being on that tour, led that year by Clive Woodward, with Gareth Jenkins and Ian McGeechan as his fellow coaches. I'd been included in the initial one hundred players of the pre-tour squad selected by Clive Woodward six months before the trip. Like the other ninety-nine, I'd received my four-coloured Lions wristband from Sir Clive, to show that I was in that select one hundred! The press that I'd read was favourable towards my selection as well, so I'd convinced myself that I was in with a fair chance of going. I had high hopes therefore, that my name would be called out by team manager Bill Beaumont on the TV, but it wasn't.

Gareth Jenkins was on the selection committee and he called me pretty much straight after the announcement had been made. I was as low as I had ever been, realising that I wasn't going to be a Lion, and, as much as I appreciated him phoning me, that feeling stayed with me throughout Gareth's call. I'm not sure if I felt worse when he told me that in the selection process Andy Robinson, Eddie O'Sullivan and Gareth himself had opted for me, but Sir Clive's casting vote meant that I was not selected. I couldn't help thinking whether a factor in Sir Clive's decision had been my turning him down when he asked me to join the England squad. I remembered watching the '93 and '97 Lions and wondering what it would be like to be involved in such a prestigious tour.

It was a very difficult time for me. Dealing with a rejection like that is not easy because you end up analysing why you weren't good enough, yet have to get on with your normal job of putting in top performances. It's difficult to hit the expected heights from such a low place; you have to jump a lot higher and work a lot harder when your reserves are low – it's not easy.

The rejection meant that I would be a part of Ireland's tour to Japan instead. Before leaving for the airport, we watched the first game of the Lions tour, against the Bay of Plenty, on the TV at the hotel. We saw a fairly comfortable Lions victory and got on the bus to Shannon airport. On that bus journey I got a phone call. Amazingly, I was called up for the Lions tour after all! I'd seen Lawrence Dallaglio suffer an ankle injury in the Bay of Plenty game on TV. It had turned out to be a serious injury, and I was called out as cover for him. To be honest, in the back of my mind, I'd half-expected to be called upon as a potential replacement for Simon Taylor who went on the tour with a hamstring niggle but, as it turned out, it was my old school peer

Lawrence Dallaglio's misfortune that proved to be my lucky break!

From then on, it was all systems go. Luckily, I was on my way to an airport, all bags were packed. But instead of going to Tokyo, I had to get a flight to Auckland. The Irish lads caught a plane to Heathrow and on to Japan. I accompanied them to Heathrow but caught a plane out to New Zealand. We said our goodbyes, I wished them luck and they were extremely supportive and encouraging towards me. It was nice to leave in that way, with the backing of the lads.

At the time, Sarra was working on a children's TV programme, *The Saturday Show*, and had been filming in Glasgow. She caught a flight back to Heathrow and through an amazing piece of luck and timing we were able to meet up in one of the world's busiest airports before I caught my flight! We had just enough time to say hello and goodbye before going our separate ways again. I then had twenty-four hours on my own to contemplate what had happened in just the last few hours, and what was ahead of me. The time proved to be very useful, as it settled my thoughts and feelings, and helped me put everything in perspective before joining the British – and Irish – Lions!

I had so many messages of good luck and support. Many mentioned the fact that I should have been selected originally. What was left for me to do, as soon as I got to New Zealand, was to prove that that should have been the case. That meant more pressure on me, but all I needed to do was think back to the time before selection, when I was playing to prove myself to the selectors. Six months had gone by since I'd received that four-coloured Lions wristband.

The goal all those months earlier had been to make the final touring squad, which, for that tour was forty-five players, far more than ever before. To cope with such a large squad, Sir Clive also took more management personnel than had ever been taken before. In the months before the announcement of the squad, there had been quite a build-up as it was led by Sir Clive, less than two years after he'd coached and managed England to a World Cup victory in the southern hemisphere. Expectations were as high as they could be. As a result, he'd been given a generous budget to prepare his squad better than any other. Everything was supposed to be bigger and better. Aspirations were certainly bigger. I was now about to join that squad and be part of making sure that the play matched the aspiration.

I was glad that I joined the Lions tour fairly early on and therefore had more of a chance to prove myself. I was on the bench for the game against the Maoris in Hamilton. They showed that they were pretty much the All Blacks' second team, and we only just beat them 19–13. I didn't get on the pitch that day. The next game was in the Cake Tin in Wellington, the Westpac Stadium, and that was my Lions debut. We won well that day, 23–6, and my own game went well too. My tour had started and I could now add being a British and Irish Lion to my CV but, of course, what I really wanted to do was play in a Test match. I still had that to aim for.

I soon realised that there were off-pitch issues on this tour, similar to the ones I was to encounter later with Ireland in 2007. To start with, even with a squad as large as forty-five players, we didn't share rooms in our hotels – and that is an essential part of touring as a

Preparing to sing 'Ireland's Call'. Always proud… but always nervous!
© Huw Evans Agency

We've done it! Success in Paris for the first time in twenty-seven years!
March 2000
© www.inpho.ie

Celebrating my first
Welsh Cup victory for
Llanelli with Stephen
Jones in May 2000
© Huw Evans Agency

Easter's Rising!
© www.inpho.ie

Celebrating winning the
Celtic League in 2003.
We beat Cardiff, 28–25

Going higher than future Scarlet
team-mate David Lyons,
World Cup 2003
© Getty Images

Lawrence Dallaligo and me – old
Amplefordians on the international stage
February 2004
© www.inpho.ie

OK… so what do I do now?
© Getty Images

Beating England was always
special – even more so in
February 2004 as they had just
been crowned World champions!
© www.inpho.ie

Celebrating Ireland's
first Triple Crown in
nine years with Malcolm
O'Kelly, February 2004

© www.inpho.ie

" … So Gareth, why did
you say Clive didn't pick
me in the original squad
for this Lions tour again?"

© www.inpho.ie

Stephen Jones, Salesi Finau and me with
the Celtic League trophy in May 2004

Two Scarlets going after All Black captain Tana Umanga, July 2005

© www.inpho.ie

Donncha and me looking dejected after losing the Lions series, July 2005

© www.inpho.ie

A 'Gidley' offload – from me… yes your eyes don't deceive you!

© www.inpho.ie

Not a bad technique… for a defensive coach!

© www.inpho.ie

Mark Jones saving my life while the opposition played on… EDF Cup final, Twickenham 2006

© www.inpho.ie

They were rare! A try v London Irish in the Heineken Cup, 2007

© Huw Evans Agency

Wales v Ireland, Drico and me congratulating Ronan on his try, February 2007

© Getty Images

My controversial tackle preventing Chris Czekaj from a certain try – Wales coaches Nigel Davies and Gareth Jenkins have never forgiven me! February 2007

© Getty Images

Battling and beating my Irish team mates in one of my proudest victories – Scarlets v Munster, Heineken Cup quarter-final, April 2007
© www.inpho.ie

On the attack versus Leicester in the Heineken Cup semi-final, 2007
© Huw Evans Agency

The closest I've come as a player to the Heineken Cup – let's hope I can go one better as a coach – Heineken Cup semi-final, April 2007
© www.inpho.ie

One of my proudest moments at Lansdowne Road – leading my country out against the All Blacks, November 2005
© www.inpho.ie

Lost for words… Eddie O'Sullivan , me, Ronan O'Gara and Malcom O'Kelly after our World Cup exit in France, November 2007

© www.inpho.ie

Bringing down one of my greatest rivals, Serge Betsen, in November 2007

© www.inpho.ie

Poor technique… for a defensive coach!

© www.inpho.ie

Leading the team out for the final game at Parc y Strade, a great send-off, beating Bristol 29–0 in front of a full house in October 2008

© Huw Evans Agency

The boys saying goodbye to the Strade faithful: me with Soffia in my arms, October 2008

Our first league match at Parc y Scarlets against Munster, November 2008

© Huw Evans Agency

Stephen Jones and me welcoming Ronan O'Gara to Stradey Park!

© www.inpho.ie

Making my point
© www.inpho.ie

"Oh sorry, was I off-side?" Martin Castrogiovani and Carlo Del Fava taking exception to me… probably being where I shouldn't be!
© www.inpho.ie

Getting past Sergio Parisse to score Ireland's fourth try in a 51–24 victory in Rome which almost won us the Championship!
© www.inpho.ie

Talking my way out of this one!

Not so lucky this time!

Guy, why is it me that's holding the dangerous end? Guy and I experiencing the wildlife during the Australia World Cup in 2003

Coming off second best to Richie McCaw! Sarra's second favourite rugby player!

Helping Dwayne and Mark drown their sorrows after beating Wales in Dublin, February 2006

Looking a bit the worse for wear – Brian O'Driscoll, Guy, me and Frankie Sheahan on a night out

Denis Hickie and me celebrating with Ronan O'Gara on his wedding day, summer 2006

Dwayne Peel, Stephen Jones, Gavin Evans, me and Regan King celebrating Steve's 30th – that was some hangover!

So how many international caps have you got again Steve? 98, 99, 100… OK you win!

Garan Evans, Barry Davies, Nigel Owens and me after a long day of cricket for the Ray Gravell Charitable Trust

"Robin, people will start talking!" Robin McBryde and me getting to grips with one another!

My toughest day on the hallowed turf – carrying Grav on to Parc y Strade for the final time

© Huw Evans Agency

One of only a handful of Irish players ever to be made into a Grogg – an honour

team. On a Lions tour you'd traditionally share a room with someone from one of the other three countries. We needed to get to know each other better as that would help us understand each other on the playing field. That bonding didn't happen. And, that was just the start. The squad was also training separately as well with, what turned out to be, the midweek Lions training apart from the weekend Lions. Gareth and Ian led the midweek sessions and Sir Clive managed the weekend squads. With games in different cities, the two squads would be flying off to different parts of New Zealand separately, as well. That split us up even more. We would go for days without seeing some of the other players. How can you gel as a team in those circumstances? That, in turn, created an 'us and them' set-up where you were either in one Lions squad or in the other. That went completely against the ethos of the Lions across the decades. The rich Lions tradition had been built on one squad coming together from four nations, bonding together and being a part of something special. Players who were part of the midweek set-up would be back-up or subs for the weekend matches as well, and those subs for the weekend would be part of the following midweek game. It was all chaotic. The 2009 Lions got things right thank goodness. But, in 2005, there was no unity or cohesion whatsoever.

Added to the forty-five player squad were over twenty management staff – that's a squad of almost seventy people. Not all of the players could understand why such a lot of managers etc. were needed in the first place. One person's selection in particular triggered a lot of discussion, Alastair Campbell, Tony Blair's former director of communications and strategy. He was there to manage TV and press relations and he also wrote a column for *The Times* during the tour. He was an easy guy to get along with, and I certainly enjoyed his company, as did many others. But, the role that he was asked to do did not sit comfortably with most of us, with one event proving to be quite negative.

We'd lost the first Test 21–3, with Woodward having probably picked the side before arriving in New Zealand. There certainly was a feeling that he hadn't considered current form when he picked the players. So, there was certain unease about that. During that game a Mealamu and Umanga spear-tackle injured Brian O'Driscoll and it meant that we'd lost our captain. But it got worse. After that first Test, Woodward decided that it would be a good idea if Alastair stood up in front of the whole squad, and gave us a talk about the pride of wearing a Lions shirt. This went down *really* badly, with the Irish players, in particular, taking exception to his talk. It was a bad move on Woodward's behalf because we felt insulted that someone who had never played any rugby was telling us about how we should be feeling as Lions. How did he know? When someone like Gareth Jenkins gave a similar talk, we could take it from him even though he'd never been a Lion, because he was a rugby man at the top level. Alastair came across as though he was questioning us as players, as individuals even. So after that first Test, we'd lost a game, our captain and the coach had lost his squad, to a large extent. Playing the Campbell card was totally counterproductive.

At that point the midweek team were winning all their games. They ended up being undefeated at the end of the tour. This again increased the 'us and them' feeling and that came to a head during the final week of the tour. We had lost both Tests by then and therefore the series. The midweek team won their last game against Auckland at Eden Park, 17–13. That led to the inevitable banter among the lads but, in this case, it was amusing banter on the surface which, however, also showed an underlying attitude which was far more serious. Matt Dawson, the England scrum-half, is always up for a laugh and he produced T-shirts for the midweek squad with 'The Midweek Massive' emblazoned on the front. On the back of the T-shirt was a list of the games they'd played and won. Matt was experienced enough, having been on two previous Lions tours, to know what being a Lion meant. He was also trying to make a point or two: we were supposed to be one Lions tour, but no one felt it was. That point wasn't aimed at the players, but at the hierarchy who had handled the tour wrongly right from the start.

On a personal level I was aware of all this, as was every other player. But, just like the others, I had to try to concentrate on my own game as well. I felt I had points to prove to my doubters, and wanted to prove Woodward wrong. You need luck in that kind of situation sometimes, and in sport it's someone else's bad luck that can bring your good fortune. Not only did Lawrence Dallaglio have to pull out with an injury, but Simon Taylor did also in the end. Lawrence stayed out there for a few weeks after I arrived, as he was having hospital treatment. We might have had our moments on the pitch, but I must say that he was a big loss for the tour. Add to that the fact that we'd lost Brian O'Driscoll as well, and Woodward had lost the two players he probably wanted to build his Test side around. Unfortunately, when those losses happened, the structure around the group dismantled to a certain extent. I missed out on the first Test, but played my way in to the last two Tests. Having not been selected in the first place, I was more than pleased with that.

When we lost Brian O'Driscoll as captain, Woodward turned to Welsh international winger Gareth Thomas to lead the tour. He did well in really difficult circumstances. One particular Alfie moment summed up the end of the tour. During the second Test in Wellington, he got us all together in a huddle to share a few words of wisdom with us, to encourage us when things weren't going well.

"Lads! Lads! We're under pressure. Our backs are against the wall. I've only got two words to say to you boys. Don't f*****g panic!"

The lads had a little laugh to themselves in a moment of real pressure, but unfortunately couldn't match the All Blacks in Wellington and we lost the game, along with the series.

I'd played against New Zealand before with the Irish team. But a Lions game contrasted greatly with taking to the field for Ireland. Everything was bigger with press conferences, for example, attended by over a hundred journalists instead of the twenty or so at internationals. This was also the Woodward Lions, and the whole circus he took with him made it bigger than ever before. But, the whole mental attitude of a Lions squad being bigger and better was also enough to motivate the All Blacks significantly too. They'd heard all the hype and bravado beforehand and they upped their game as a result. We probably played against one of the best ever All Black teams.

So, it was back on the plane, but now I was a fully-fledged Lion. When I look back on my career, I'm sure it's that fact that will be paramount in my mind, the experience of wearing that special shirt. At the end of the day, I have plenty of good memories that I'll always keep with me.

17

A Tale of Two Stadiums

I'VE BEEN LUCKY enough to play my sport in about thirteen different countries around the world – and at some of the best rugby stadiums. But there are two rugby venues which mean a lot to me, mostly for reasons other than rugby itself. They are places where rugby, history, community, passion and personality have come together. Not surprisingly, one is in Ireland and the other is in Wales.

Sunday, the 21st of November, 1920 was a black day in Irish history. Tipperary were playing Dublin in the Great Challenge match. But it wasn't rugby; it was a Gaelic football match played at Croke Park, or Croker as it's known to Dubliners. The site, fifteen minutes from Dublin city centre, had been the stronghold of the Gaelic Athletic Association (GAA) since 1884. But that particular day wasn't about Gaelic football either. On that Sunday, the Royal Irish Constabulary and the English Auxiliary Division entered the ground during the match and indiscriminately shot at the crowd. Fourteen people were killed – thirteen spectators and the Tipperary captain, Michael Hogan. That day was the first Bloody Sunday and the action of the police and military was in revenge for the killing of fourteen British intelligence officers by Michael Collins' IRA. It was the period of the Irish War of Independence and Croke Park became a symbol of all things republican, a visual focus reflecting the battle between the Irish and the English establishment. In 1924, when the ground was developed further, the main stand was named the Hogan Stand.

When the home of the Irish Rugby Football Union, Lansdowne Road, needed to be closed for redevelopment, Croke Park was chosen as its temporary replacement. As a stadium, it is superb, and it's the largest stadium in Europe not used for football. But, the GAA was founded as a nationalist organisation to promote all things Irish in the sporting arena. Gaelic football and hurling were conceived as a sporting objection to all things British. On the one hand, that has meant that it's been embraced by the Irish as a means of safeguarding all things indigenously Irish. And, on the other hand, it has refused to embrace any sport deemed to be foreign to its influence. The agreement to host rugby matches there was, therefore, genuinely historic. And that was even truer for the second rugby international game ever to be played there. That game was against England, which brought the events of eighty years ago flooding back. The big question was would 'God Save the Queen' be sung there? It had been the subject of heated debate for months before the game. Many saw the hosting of rugby union games at Croke Park as an insult and an inflammatory gesture. Others, however, saw it as a chance to be proud of all things Irish and to celebrate our identity on a bigger stage. Certainly, the GAA didn't need financially to agree to the stadium being used for rugby union and football at that time. Therefore, the agreement to do so came from a position of strength on their behalf, not weakness. As it turned out, the anthem was sung, and respected by the Irish supporters who remained silent throughout. That was a huge sign of respect considering that the vast majority of Irish fans in the stadium would have known full well about the Bloody Sunday atrocity.

The first game at Croke Park was against France and we narrowly lost to a last-minute Vincent Clerc try. The most memorable thing for me was Paul O'Connell's speech in the dressing room before the game. He reminded us of where we were playing and the history associated with it. He was the man to do that, and it came from his heart.

And then the England game came around. I've never known such a build-up in the week preceding a match. We certainly realised that it was actually more than just a rugby match. We felt as if we were playing for the Irish rugby loving public of course. But on that day, we also sensed that we were playing for the whole of Ireland regardless of whether they liked rugby or not. We'd had the feeling all week that we were just meant to beat England on such an historic day. Call it a sense of destiny or whatever, but that's how it was. The pressure was all on England that day.

While all this historical discussion surrounding an 80-minute game of rugby on the Saturday afternoon was going on, I had my own personal issues to deal with. Sarra, who was by then my wife, was expecting our first child. On the Tuesday before the game, I got a call from her to say that she was going into labour and that I had better get back home as soon as I could. Luckily for me,

Ronan O'Gara had a friend who owned a helicopter and he flew me back to Cardiff after I'd had permission to leave the Irish camp. The hope was that the baby would be born, I could also avoid all the attention and controversy surrounding the game, and I'd be able to get back just in time to play the match itself. When I got back to south Wales, it turned out to be a false alarm and Sarra was OK. The only problem was having to go back to the squad, face the lads and tell them that the birth hadn't happened after all! They gave me a hard time, but it was all in good spirit! When I got back I learned that Brian O'Driscoll was fit to play, which was great, but the main discussion point was still the anthem. When 'God Save the Queen' was sung and greeted with the respect mentioned earlier, the England captain Martin Corry said how much the England players appreciated the gesture.

On the pitch, we played our best rugby for a while and had our biggest victory against England, beating them 43–13. It just had to be and it was a phenomenal day. There was a fair bit of emotion flying around the changing room after the game – spirits were high and feelings were deep. We'd won a rugby game but there was also a sense of putting a chapter of history to bed as well.

I phoned Sarra after the game and she was still OK in terms of the pregnancy. Coming from rugby pedigree herself, and being Welsh, she understood the significance of the day and the game and was rejoicing with me. She told me to go out and celebrate with the lads and, of course, I just had to listen to her! As a squad, we stuck together that night more than we'd done for a while because we just knew that we had to.

Four o'clock on the Sunday morning, feeling slightly fragile, Sarra phoned. She'd gone into labour! My head was by then all over the place! But I knew I needed to get back to Wales as soon as I could. But there was no helicopter this time. The hotel was fantastic and sorted everything for me. I got a flight back at 1 p.m. that afternoon to Bristol, got a taxi to the Princess of Wales Hospital, Bridgend, and walked in there at 4.30 p.m. Sarra gave birth to Soffia, our first child, at 5.10 p.m! I was on cloud nine the day before at Croke Park. I've no idea what number cloud I was on when I witnessed the birth of my first child a day later!

Croke Park will forever have a very special place in my heart for what was the perfect weekend for me. The importance of the game was not lost on any of the Irish players. And that followed by the birth of my first child! It really was a weekend of history, destiny, drama and fulfilment. When Soffia was born, the words of the great Welsh legend, Ray Gravell, came back to me. He told me once that no matter what I did in my rugby career, whatever I achieved, nothing was more important than the birth of your children.

Little did I know that just over six months after that momentous weekend, I would be at the funeral of the great Grav. Much like the first, my second special rugby venue is chosen for reasons other than just the rugby itself.

Ray Gravell played for Llanelli 485 times between 1969 and 1985, scoring 120 tries. He captained the side from 1980 to 1982. He played for Wales 23 times and won two Grand Slams, four Five Nations Championships and four Triple Crowns. He was a British and Irish Lion. The slogan 'Gravell eats soft centres' was coined for him.

It would be enough to end listing Grav's achievements there. But he was so much more than just a rugby player. He captured the heart of the whole of Wales, both Welsh speaking and non-Welsh speaking, such was his infectious personality.

From the minute I arrived at Llanelli, Ray was an ever-present personality. He was always somewhere in the corridors of Stradey Park, enthusing about something that was on his mind, encouraging someone he came across or sharing his passion for all things Welsh. He was literally a presence bigger than the physical space he occupied. In 2007, diabetes got the better of him, and he had to have his lower leg amputated. Ever the positive personality, he inspired everyone with his remarkable recovery from such a trauma. His prosthetic leg was emblazoned with the Scarlets' logo and he wore shorts to make sure everyone saw it. There was no hiding behind self-pity or long trousers for Grav.

At times during his illnesses, Grav didn't come to Stradey Park. We all really missed him. For me, as captain, I missed his wisdom and his guidance. But then he came back, in his wheelchair, and still with the same presence. The lads warmed even more to the spirit he showed after his illness. One thing he had done repeatedly over the years was to come into the changing room before a game. When he did this, he would often note the various watches worn by the players. In particular, he loved Alix Popham's watch, always asking to see it and have explained what it could do.

As a gesture, the players decided to club together and buy him a watch to show him how we felt about him. Three of us, Alix Popham, Gavin Thomas and I, went to his home in Mynydd y garreg to present him with the engraved watch. On the balcony outside his home, overlooking his beloved village with Kidwelly in the distance, we gave him the watch and his response was characteristically emotional. Some time earlier, he'd come on to the pitch at Stradey in his wheelchair accompanied by his two daughters, Manon and Gwenan. Such a show of courage left its mark on the players – he always had a huge hold over them. But that year, there seemed to be a special affinity due to his illness.

As October 2007 approached, the talk was again about the anniversary of the famous Scarlets victory against the All Blacks in October 1972. Grav played in that team, as did my former coach Gareth Jenkins. Thirty-five years to the day of that momentous victory, we heard the news that Grav had died of a heart attack while on holiday with his family in Spain. We were all stunned, as was the whole of Wales. Grav was the constant in the Scarlets players' lives, as he was for so many other people. Now, that continuum was gone.

Not long afterwards, I got a phone call from the chairman of one of the Scarlets' main sponsors, WRW, asking me if I was prepared to be one of the bearers during Grav's funeral. I told Robert Williams that it was the deepest honour to be asked, but it gave me a huge dilemma. I wanted to say yes but I felt wrong in saying so. I shouldn't have had to say yes because it wasn't right that he'd passed away. There was a confusion of thoughts in my head. I couldn't believe that I would never again experience the warmth of his wonderful personality. How his wife and children coped with their loss, I have no idea.

I then learned that the funeral would be held at Stradey Park itself. My role would be, with others, to carry the great man onto the pitch at Stradey, where the funeral service would take place. It was unusual to have a funeral at a rugby stadium. Which other man in Welsh life would anyone think of honouring in that way? No one.

The funeral procession arrived at Stradey and Ray's coffin was taken into the changing room, and he was left there alone for a few minutes behind closed doors. Then, the bearers went into the changing room and we stayed there for a few minutes with Ray's coffin. We stood there: Stephen Jones, Dwayne Peel, myself, and his former team mates from the '70s Scarlets and Wales team: Derek Quinnell, Gareth Jenkins and Delme Thomas. I will never forget that feeling of grieving, respectful silence in a changing room that had seen legends come and go for well over a century. And there was Ray, ready to leave that same changing room for the last time.

The time came for us to carry the coffin out onto the pitch. The experience in the changing room gave me one strong emotion, walking onto the pitch gave me another. I was used to walking out onto a rugby pitch in front of thousands of people. I was used to the Lansdowne roar, the cacophony of sound in Paris, the intensity and passion of Welsh crowds. But I had *never* experienced anything like this: we walked out to face ten thousand silent people. It was chilling. Some wore black, some wore Grav's replica shirts, and others wore the trademark Grav red scarf and gloves.

We proceeded across the pitch towards those who were to take part in the service: Burry Port Brass Band, Llanelli Male Voice Choir, former Archdruid of Wales Meirion Evans, rugby legend Gerald Davies, Welsh literary giant Professor Hywel Teifi Edwards, Welsh folk legend Dafydd Iwan, singer-songwriter Gwyneth Glyn and Wales' First Minister, Rhodri Morgan – representatives of Welsh public and popular life whom Grav had touched and inspired, symbols of the scope of his influence. They were all, also, his personal friends. Behind us were the ones who carried the heaviest burden of grief and loss, his wife Mari and two young daughters, Manon, eleven and Gwenan, eight.

One particular indication of Grav's influence and the esteem in which he was held was the presence of my former team-mate, Welsh international and British Lion, Robin McBryde. For years before he was taken ill, Ray was what's known as the Keeper of the Sword at the premier Welsh cultural event, the National Eisteddfod. This role is a ceremonial one and it dates back to the beginning of the nineteenth century. This massive sword is always carried at the main Eisteddfod events by its blade, not by its grip, to signify the predominantly pacifist tradition of Welsh culture. When Ray was taken ill and could no longer fulfil this function, Robin McBryde was chosen as his successor. For the first time in almost 200 years, the Eisteddfod officials had an emergency meeting and agreed to let the sword be used for the first time outside the Eisteddfod field. It was an immense honour – such was the respect shown to the great Ray Gravell. Robin stood there, bearing the sword, without flinching, for the whole ceremony.

Stradey Park was Grav's place of worship. He was a man who kept the faith with everyone he came across. It was so fitting, therefore, that he was laid to rest in his spiritual home with the whole of Wales and the rugby world looking on. No one else would have commanded such an outpouring of emotion and support on such a scale. For me, as a non-Welshman, I really *got* what it was to be Welsh, through Grav. He embraced his culture without alienating those who weren't a part of it. The day of Grav's funeral will stay with me for ever.

Both Croke Park and Stradey Park have, in their own way, fulfilled the same function. Both have been symbols of national identity. In Croke Park's case, a symbol in the face of bloody opposition and conflict, but the symbol also of a nation which had moved on from the past with a sense of pride and confidence. Stradey Park was a symbol of a whole nation uniting to honour one of its sons who so firmly believed in the sense of identity that rugby, more than any other sport, gave to his beloved Wales. For me, both stadiums on both occasions showed clearly that, every now and then, rugby can be about so much more than just thirty men running around a field.

18

Old Roots and New Shoots

It seems another world away now – my time as a farm hand on my dad's farm and turning out for Harrogate on weekends. I've just recounted all the varying chapters of my life: I've won sixty-five caps for Ireland and played in two Lions Tests, I've played over 200 games for the Scarlets and was captain for five seasons – and let's not forget nearly twenty tries as well! But now, a new chapter is opening out in front of me, as I get to grips with a coaching role at Parc y Scarlets. I've had to overcome quite a lot in my rugby career, not least the serious injuries. Now I have to prove myself in a different rugby arena. But yesterday's successes are no guarantee that I will succeed tomorrow.

I suppose that my seasons as club captain helped me develop man-management skills, but now that has been taken to a completely new level, as I am responsible for the rugby development of so many individual players, and their performance as team Scarlets. I've played under some fantastic coaches over the years including

John Willcox, Phil Davies and Gareth Jenkins in key developmental stages of my career. Fortunately, I have their legacy to draw upon as well. That's not a bad start! Coming to Llanelli, quite honestly, was not a long-term part of my life plan. At the time, I saw it as a means to an end, to further my ambitions, but the club has had an incredible hold on me. I stayed, but I could easily have moved on to begin my coaching career elsewhere. It's always a tough decision when you stay at your club, as it can be interpreted as just a case of jobs for the boys. On the other hand, however, if a club lets you leave and you coach somewhere else, they are criticised for not using their own talent to further the game. It's best to ignore that kind of argument, otherwise you end up going round in circles. Coaching is a challenge for me, because I have to get used to the feeling that, as soon as the players have crossed the whitewash, I can't do very much and it's then up to them. I prepare them to be as good as they can be, once they cross that line. I feel very fortunate that Nigel and the Scarlets have given me the opportunity to coach at the highest level. So many players leave the game straight after finishing playing, and struggle to adjust to normal life. At Scarlets we have a young coaching group in Mark Jones, Vernon Cooper and myself, with also the experience of Gareth Potter (head analyst), Brad Harrington (head of strength and conditioning) and Nigel at the helm, pulling it all together. Over the last couple of years we've promoted from within: on the management side, ex-Scarlet and Welsh international wing, Garan Evans, is also team manager. And on the playing front, we are now seeing the benefits of that development, and if we can keep hold of these young, talented players, the future is most definitely going to be bright, if not scarlet!

I'd only been at the Scarlets for about six months or so, when I attended a charity fashion show at a local television studio, where a few of the Scarlets boys had been asked to model. A rather attractive blonde-haired young lady caught my eye; we had a chance to exchange some pleasantries and that was it. Well, sort of. The problem was I couldn't stop seeing her. But, she never saw me though. At the time, she was presenting a Welsh children's TV programme and advertising billboards for the programme, with her picture on them were to be seen all around Cardiff. I'd mentioned several times to Guy and Rhodri Davies, who shared a house with me in Cardiff, that I really fancied the girl on the billboard. They, of course, started to tease me and they both said that I would end up going out with her. But there was no contact between us at that time.

Then, one night in Cardiff, Sarra turned up with some of her friends at the bar where we were drinking. This was almost a year since that first brief encounter at the charity fashion event. That night, I was wearing a bright yellow Hawaiian shirt and had died my hair peroxide blonde, so I sort of stood out from the crowd anyway! This didn't put her off thankfully and we got chatting, shared a few drinks and got on really well. So well, in fact, that we got to the exchanging phone numbers stage! The following day, Sarra was off to London for the week with work and I was flying back to Ireland to prepare to play against Scotland in a rearranged international due to the foot and mouth outbreak earlier that year. We spoke a lot that week and when I returned to Wales, we went on our first date to an Italian in Cardiff Bay and started seeing a lot of each other. After a few months, we decided to have a break from each other. It was all down to me, as I didn't want to get too serious too soon... how quickly I realised that this wasn't actually what I wanted! Grav got to hear about the split and did his best, in his own inimitable way, to basically tell me not to be so stupid and to get back with her straightaway! "Think of the babies" he said. "They'll be able to play for Ireland and Wales!" Unbeknown to me, he had also seen Sarra and told her that we needed to get back together again pretty quickly, and told her in no uncertain terms what a mistake we were making! An unlikely Cupid, but a successful one, and it was a pleasure to invite Grav and his wife Mari to our wedding!

Having been an item for a few weeks, Sarra took me to meet her parents – scary for any prospective boyfriend, but made even more so by the fact that her father, Elgan, is a former Welsh, British and Irish Lion and a Neath legend. But from the moment I met Elgan and Kathryn, any worries I had soon disappeared! Sarra and her parents are very close and they quickly made me feel like part of the family. Sarra also fitted into my family very well, so much so that when we had our 'break', Elgan and Kathryn took my side, and my mum and dad took Sarra's!

After three years together I plucked up the courage (and not before time, Sarra would say!) in the good old-fashioned way and went to see Elgan to ask him for permission to marry his daughter. Even with me fluffing my well-rehearsed lines, he said yes. But more importantly, so did Sarra. I asked her to marry me in the pouring rain on a building site! Not any old building site, I hasten to add, but our future half-built marital home, a converted barn which overlooks beautiful views of the Vale of Glamorgan and north Devon! Not the most romantic of locations I grant you – but I guess you had to be there! I'm so lucky to have Sarra in my life; she's a beautiful person inside and out, a wonderful wife, even though her cooking needs a little work! She has given me two of the most beautiful children. Sometimes we go through life without appreciating what we have, and lose sight of what's most important. Love, health, happiness and family are all we really need – anything else is a bonus.

We got engaged in 2004 and married the following year. That summer was amazing, a Lions tour and our wedding, all within a couple of weeks of each other. The weekend of the wedding was fantastic. We hired Llangoed Hall near Brecon for the entire weekend and the celebrating started on the Friday night before we took our vows on Saturday afternoon. The big day was awesome – seeing Sarra walk up the aisle was incredible, she looked perfect. We always spoke of her not being able to hold it together, but it was Elgan and myself who let emotion get the better of us! After a beautiful service at St Mary's church in Builth Wells, we headed back to Llangoed Hall for the reception. Llangoed Hall is an amazing country house which dates back over 400 years and, even here, there's no escaping the Irish. The mansion was owned by the McNamara family about 200 years ago; they'd won the stately building in a game of cards! More recently, it was redesigned by Sir Clough Williams-Ellis, the architect responsible for the Italianate village at Portmeirion, Porthmadog, and was turned into a hotel in 1990 by Bernard Ashley, husband of Laura. We filled it with family and friends and everything was organised by Sarra and her mum Kathryn to the finest detail.

I had three best men on the day, Stephen Jones, Matt Cardey and Guy, who did get me to the church on time. However, I missed so much of the run-up to the weekend, because I was away with the Lions. I got back from that tour on the 13th of July and the wedding was set for the 30th, so there wasn't much to do by the time I got back! There was plenty of time, however, to fit in a stag do; that was essential. We had a really good time in Nottingham, spending a whole day, as part of that weekend, watching the Australian cricket team play Leicestershire in a four-day warm-up match before the Ashes Tests. I was, of course, dressed up by my friends, who had decided that I was to be the wheelchair-bound Andy from the Andy and Lou sketch on *Little Britain*. Chris Wyatt had somehow got hold of an old wheelchair, which looked big and awkward. So, I was pushed around in this all day. Fortunately, in one way, a friend of Guy's had organised a hospitality suite for us at the cricket and we had that to ourselves.

During one of the intervals, the public were given an opportunity to bowl some balls on a corner of the pitch. I was wheeled out and placed there by whoever Lou was at that time. Then, when he walked away, just as on *Little Britain*, I would get out of my wheelchair and bowl a ball at the wicket before running back to my chair by the time Lou came back. The crowd loved it and it went down very well. It was also nice to say that I'd bowled a few balls during an Australian cricket match!

I actually went one better than that, and found my way up to the Australian dressing room. Guy and I just walked past whoever was at the bottom of the stairs leading up to the dressing room and knocked on the door. The door opened and there they all were, sitting around during the tea interval.

"Isn't it time you retired, Ricky?" was my question to the legendary Australian captain, Ricky Ponting. I had a fair bit of abuse back, as you can imagine, and a withering look from Shane Warne as he took another drag on his cigarette, which had a 'who the "f" are you mate?' kind of feel to it. I was asked to leave. I apologised as I walked away, and wished them good luck. England went on to win the Ashes later that summer. I always feel that I had a small part to play in that victory with my small, slightly intoxicated intervention on behalf of English cricket!

After the wedding, Sarra and I went to a small, quiet boutique hotel in northern Greece for our honeymoon. One night, Sarra and I were sat in the hotel bar and she was looking over my shoulder now and again at one of the other guests. She asked me if I knew who this guy was but I had no idea! We left it at that. Not long afterwards, we were having a glass of wine with the hotel's owner and Sarra asked him who that guy she thought she recognised was. He said that he was Domenico Dolce, one half of the world-famous Italian design house Dolce and Gabbana. Sarra was ecstatic! It was Sarra's birthday that day too, and the owner brought out a cake for her and made it a really nice occasion. After the cake had been presented to Sarra, and the entire restaurant had embarrassed her by singing 'Happy birthday', we heard a voice from behind us say, "Do you mind if we join you for a drink?" It was Domenico and his boyfriend! We didn't mind at all and we shared the cake with them and had a few drinks before we moved on to another bar. In the end we spent quite a bit of time with them, and it really made Sarra's birthday to have a fashion icon share the night with her. I would have loved to have been able to claim that I had organised it all. I tried, of course, but it didn't work!

On our return home, it was time to settle in to married life. We had already decided to move out of Cardiff to the Vale of Glamorgan. Our barn conversion was finished and all the hard work of being involved in the process from beginning to end was worth it! Part of the thinking about moving away from city life was that we both wanted to start a family. One afternoon, I went out for a run and returned to find a distraught Sarra standing on the doorstep asking me why I hadn't answered my mobile, as she'd been calling me since I'd left! The simple answer was that I don't take my phone with me on a run. She then told me that she'd been phoning to say that we were expecting – she was pregnant! We were over the moon – we both sat there for what seemed like ages, crying tears of joy. We hadn't had to wait a year after getting married to hear those words. Our beautiful baby girl, Soffia, was born on the 25th of February, on the weekend of Ireland's game against England at Croke Park, which I mentioned earlier.

So it was a case of a new wife, new home, and new baby and she was amazing! Nothing can prepare you for becoming a parent – that feeling of complete and utter unconditional love that you have for your child, from the very first moment you set eyes on your baby – it's like nothing I've ever experienced. Two years later I was to experience those feelings again when our son,

Ffredi, was born. And, it wasn't travelling home for the birth in time from a match, which caused the problems this time (I was there with Sarra throughout the labour), but it was Ffredi's size that raised eyebrows! Ffredi was born on the 1st of May, 2009 at the Princess of Wales Hospital at... wait for it... 10lb 15oz!

Our kids are my greatest achievement in life – they are truly amazing. Words cannot begin to describe how much they are loved. They're funny, kind, and bright. Soffia is wise beyond her years and Ffredi is a real character. Having children puts everything else in perspective. Like any professional sportsman, I hate losing, but when you come home to your family there is a sense of 'it's just a game'. Nothing else matters but them.

Family is everything now – what would I be without them? Here in Wales, Sarra and the kids, her mum, dad and mam-gu Marianne, and of course my family back home – mum, my sister Debs, her husband Chris and my brother Guy, who now divides his time between Yorkshire and Dublin where he lives with his girlfriend Laurie. I love them all dearly, and I would be nothing without their love, support and guidance. I also have a niece and two nephews now who are wonderful – Francesca, Sebastian, Toby and their sister Charlotte who are Debs and Chris' children. It's so important to me that they all grow up to have a close bond – we spend as much time together as possible. They come down here on school holidays and we go up there when breaks in the season allow. I love seeing them together. My sister and I have become quite emotional in our old age and it means so much to us that are all so close.

Sarra, Soffia and Ffredi have been the link between my upbringing and the new family that I am a part of.

They have also changed me as a person. I have grown to understand family life in a totally new way. I've learned to show my feelings.

There have been a number of quite significant endings in my life in the last few years and these have made me ask some questions. I've now retired from playing for Ireland, but does that mean I'm no longer Irish? No. It's not just pulling on the rugby jersey of the Emerald Isle that makes me Irish, and I didn't stop being an Irishman once I hung up my boots. Mum's family line is still there, tying me firmly to Ireland. I haven't lived in Yorkshire for years and my link to my English ancestry, my father, has passed away. Does that mean I'm no longer a Yorkshireman either? No, of course it doesn't. The farm remains in the family, ensuring the continuation of that line as well. I still embrace both historical family influences on me.

Maybe there's another unseen influence in my life as well. Sarra's maternal grandfather, her Dat-cu Brynaman – Howard, passed away a few months before Sarra and I met, while on a weekend away with Sarra's gran, Marianne, at the Cheltenham races. One of Howard's passions was horse racing, and he had also played scrum-half for, believe it or not, Llanelli Rugby Club in the 1950s! Sarra always says that he would have been so glad that his granddaughter had married a man who, not only came from a horse racing family, but who played for Llanelli's Scarlets! Sarra says that her grandfather was looking down on us when we met, and his passing was part of the process of bringing us together. So, to that rich vein of heritage in my life, I can also add the guiding hand of fate – if a Catholic boy is allowed to talk in terms of fate!

169

But, I have a new focus now. I hadn't visited Wales before I was twenty. Today, I have two children with a Welsh-speaking mum and we bring them up to speak that language. They are educated in it, they play in it. Sarra and I spend much of our time in Welsh-speaking circles, although I haven't got to grips with the language myself yet, but I am trying! I embrace this new identity that we're creating together. It's a continuation, a moving on, and a building on the foundations of what's gone before. And, in Ffredi and Soffia, I have the eternal hope that this rich heritage will continue in a brand new way.

He has made his mark both here in Wales and across the rugby world as one of the most respected players of this or any other generation.

Ieuan Evans

He's a typical flanker – he has no fear, he isn't afraid to go in where it hurts, and he's got the face to prove it!

Scott Quinnell

He has a huge determination and his attitude is simple – he's not prepared to compromise.

Gareth Jenkins

Simon has made a lot of sacrifices over the years to play for Ireland and he's earned the respect of his fellow players, even if he is a nightmare to play against!

Paul O'Connell

Simon has done a lot for Llanelli and Irish rugby and has consistently been at the forefront of both teams' efforts in what is a demanding position in an extremely attritional sport.

Ronan O'Gara

In this professional era, Simon has adopted the highest standards and he has always played with the great mind and enthusiasm of the great Irish players of former generations.

Jean-Pierre Rives

I used to share a room with him, something I won't miss! He is the biggest neatness freak I have ever come across!

Geordan Murphy

Simon's leadership, commitment and skill throughout his career has been exceptional. Whether he was wearing the colours of Llanelli Scarlets, Ireland or the British and Irish Lions, his devotion to the cause as been unquestioned.

Michael Lynagh

If I had to sum up Simon, that would be simple – honest and loyal.

Phil Davies

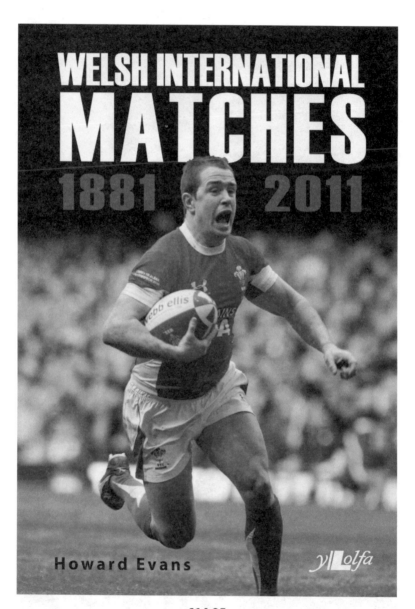

WELSH INTERNATIONAL
MATCHES
1881   2011

Howard Evans

y Lolfa

£14.95

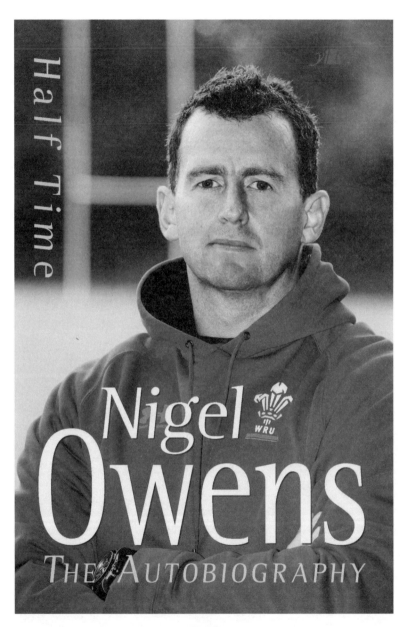

Half Time

Nigel
Owens
THE AUTOBIOGRAPHY

£9.95